Also by the author

One of Ours: Timothy McVeigh and the Oklahoma City Bombing

MY GRANDFATHER'S
PRISON

MY GRANDFATHER'S PRISON

A STORY OF DEATH AND DECEIT
IN 1940s KANSAS CITY

RICHARD A. SERRANO

UNIVERSITY OF MISSOURI PRESS
COLUMBIA AND LONDON

Library of Congress Cataloging-in-Publication Data

Serrano, Richard A.
  My grandfather's prison : a story of death and deceit in 1940s
Kansas City / Richard A. Serrano.
     p. cm.
  Summary: "Author discovers the fate of the grandfather he never
knew, who had abruptly abandoned his family during the Great
Depression, become a prisoner to alcohol and skid row, and, en-
tangled in the corrupt Pendergast era of Kansas City, Missouri, had
finally been murdered at the old Kansas City Municipal Farm"—
Provided by publisher.
  ISBN 978-0-8262-1864-3 (alk. paper)
  1. Lyons, James P., 1908-1948. 2. Murder—Missouri—Kansas
City. 3. Murder victims—Missouri—Kansas City. 4. Murder investigation—Missouri—Kansas City. 5. Alcoholics—Missouri—Kansas
City—Biography. 6. Political corruption—Missouri—Kansas City—
History—20th century. 7. Kansas City (Mo.)—Politics and govern-
ment. 8. Kansas City (Mo.)—Biography. I. Title.
  HV6534.K2S44 2009
  364.152'3092—dc22

                                                    2009013878

⊚™ This paper meets the requirements of the
American National Standard for Permanence of Paper
for Printed Library Materials, Z39.48, 1984.

Designer & Typesetter: Aaron Lueders
Printer and binder: Thomson–Shore, Inc.
Typefaces: Palatino, Cargo D, Stone Sans ITC

To my mother,

Mary Elizabeth Lyons Serrano

MY GRANDFATHER'S
PRISON

CHAPTER 1

The guard shined the flashlight along the wall, searching through the predawn darkness for the prisoner in the basement, finding him crumpled on the floor. For twenty-five hours the man had been held in solitary confinement, in what the inmates called the Hole and the guards the Dungeon. The jail staff had given him a bare mattress for comfort, and a bucket for his waste. Now the spotlight found him facedown, his body covered with bruises, his neck broken. He was thirty-nine years old.

I never knew my grandfather. I was born five years after he died in May 1948 at the old Municipal Farm, then the Kansas City jail, an imposing old castle that housed mostly drunks plucked from the streets and put to work planting corn and beans, and slopping hogs. Pay a fifteen-dollar fine or serve fifteen days.

My mother never knew her father, either. He vanished when she was two or three, taking off at the height of the Great Depression. She bore his Irish name—Lyons—but could tell us little about the man. That is because her mother, my grandmother, was resigned to forgetting about James Lyons. All she would say was that he had died years ago at the old jail. "A lovable drunk," she might tell us in dismissing her former husband. Or recall with a grin how he poured Irish whiskey into his morning coffee. Once at a baseball game, she turned to my mother and pointed at a vendor working the aisles. "That's your father," she said.

When my grandmother died we buried the secret with her. Then my mother grew ill, and as the years passed she would occasionally wonder aloud, "If you could find out something . . ." Her brother, a Kansas City lawyer, tried once to uncover the story of their father but got nowhere. Eventually he died, and my mother followed him, and when they were gone a surprising thing happened.

1

We discovered in boxes of old family memorabilia a loose photograph, stuffed with other pictures and frayed documents announcing births and baptisms, weddings and funerals. The snapshot is in black-and-white, and it shows two couples standing in a field somewhere, or perhaps a backyard in the city. All are attired formally, the men in suits and ties, the women in dresses. The photographer is shooting them from behind the sun, so they are squinting at us.

On the back is a date, 1930, the year my grandparents were married. The couple on the left is a Mr. and Mrs. Geer, totally unknown to us. They are clearly intoxicated, slouching, their hair disheveled, stumbling against one another. On the right are Mr. and Mrs. Lyons: my grandmother Zillah and her husband, James. She alone is beaming at the camera, her smile wide, and her eyes bright and fearless in the harsh sun. He, however, is squinting, or is it just his narrow eyes, thin like his long mouth? He wears a dark suit and buttoned-down vest, his shoulders erect, projecting an air of self-confidence. He is taller than the rest; he appears almost to be holding up the others. He seems the strong one.

He was twenty-two then, and had not yet disappeared into the bottle. Alcoholism eventually would become the other prison from which James Lyons could not escape, the other solitary confinement that would cost him jobs and wives and children, and grandchildren too, and send him to the jail that closed out his life. Looking again at the photograph, you can almost sense that he is bracing himself, that he knows hard times are coming.

We filed the photograph away in our shoe box of family history, stuffed for a while in a cabinet drawer, later atop a closet shelf. Then recently I dragged it out one more time, after happening upon old Missouri death records that now are made available on the Internet. There to my horror—and yes, shame—I first learned about my grandfather's end. He died from "shock . . . fractured neck . . . traumatic conditions . . ." His crime: drunk in public.

So I went looking for him. I searched inside the limestone caves along the Missouri River where old city and county records are warehoused, in public libraries poring over microfilmed city directories and histories of skid row, in the ornate reading room of the Library of Congress in Washington, reading transcripts of Senate hearings into Kansas City corruption in the late 1940s. I unfolded old newspapers, the *Kansas City Star* and its morning edition, the

Kansas City Times, where I cut my teeth as a reporter and where those after me, fortunately, saved clippings from their daily printed diary of the town where I was born.

I learned that Farm inmates worked in chain gangs and often were fed soppy bread and water, and that guards were woefully ill-equipped to care for prisoners. A series of grand juries complained about conditions there, warning that a tragedy lurked inside the jailhouse walls. The sheriff's office assigned to investigate the death was equally inept: fat, lazy deputies bought by low-level hoodlums. The sheriff himself was believed to be on the take. Then there was the sheriff's homicide unit, ridiculed across Missouri for its incompetence. True to their reputation, they proved unable or unwilling to figure out who turned the key on that Dungeon door and who might have broken my grandfather's neck for him.

Alcohol, divorce, prison, and a jailhouse death, dishonor too—these were the tragedies of my grandfather's life. For months I hunted for clues into what had happened to him, repeatedly returning from Washington to Kansas City in search of answers, and along the way I encountered a parade of characters who crossed his path. Many of them he undoubtedly knew. Some he knew quite well.

Street bums like my grandfather hovered on skid row, a neglected, scalded area near the river bottom that had once housed the city's gilded community. He and the other drunks staggered down back alleys, and slept it off in the bushes or behind trash bins. One boasted he could drink seventy-five whiskies in a single day. Others were hauled away in police paddy wagons, often scores at a time, my grandfather eighty times for vagrancy and public intoxication. His friend and roommate, an untamed, unshorn, unmarried fellow Irishman, walked persistently up and down Fifth and Main streets. He was my grandfather's last roommate, and he was the king of skid row.

A local mortician with a funeral parlor on the city's impoverished West Side buried many of the city's poor, and he chronicled their short lives and often untimely ends in a large, bound leather book he kept in his office. He buried a former circus trapeze artist who in his last years sold newspapers on the street, and he took to her rest a two-year-old girl who one afternoon wandered off into the Blue River. He also in the spring of 1948 opened a back room to his funeral parlor and during a medical autopsy helped the county coroner and the city's most respected pathologist discover the true cause of my grandfather's death.

That year was a great crossroads for Kansas City. In the period after World War II the city was finally unbridling the yoke of the Pendergast political machine, and many of the top political officials who made decisions about my grandfather's case continued to serve as the old boss's longtime protégés. They still marched to his banner, still tried to blow a spark on the cold ashes of the former regime. Some that summer of '48 were locked in desperate political battles and fighting for their own careers—all of which they quickly deemed more important than investigating who might have killed a hopeless drunk in a basement jail cell. So when officialdom declined to take up my grandfather's death as a homicide, it fell to a less-than-perfect coroner-inquest jury system to try to make sense of the broken neck and the body filled with cuts and bruises.

Despite the efforts to cover up his death, the one thing I learned above all others was this: my grandfather did not kill himself.

I dug deeper. I discovered a city filled with lost souls like James Lyons. If the bottle was not their undoing, then it was drugs or divorce or depression, or suicide. Some leaped from railroad bridges and hospital windows. One was so frightened of being sent to the Kansas City Municipal Farm that he tossed himself out of the eighth floor of police headquarters. Another jumped twice hoping to end his life, after the first time merely breaking his back did not do the trick.

I read about prisoners dashing for freedom with deep bruises up their legs from iron chains that clanged behind them, of prison food that often amounted to nothing more than bread and water, of inmates working the corn, wheat, and onion fields under the noontime glare of guards armed with shotguns.

And I read the front pages of the newspapers and the police reports at headquarters, often splattered with the details of unsolved murders, spot killings, and mob contracts. Many of the senseless deaths were sparked not so much by a finger poised at the trigger as by the alcohol in the bloodstream. My grandfather's death became just another small black notch in a city trying to get beyond its reputation as a wide-open town of booze, bimbos, and big bands, and the long dark years of boss control and the Great Depression.

I even uncovered to my further shame the story of my grandfather's one brother, Joseph Lyons Jr., a three-time loser who like him was a-swim in a bottle of whiskey, and who lay wasting away in a prison infirmary in Kansas.

My journey for my grandfather ended on a sloping hill in a local cemetery, what the gravediggers call "the Old Section" because its ground was opened sixty years ago, in a lot where few come to visit anymore. I gazed down at the flat headstone at my feet, "James P. Lyons, 1908–1948." The image in that worn photograph had brought me here. As my family says, I look just like him.

CHAPTER 2

I grew up in a family without grandparents. My father came from Mexico, and his father, a poor, devout Catholic, died before I started school. I never set eyes on him. My father's mother, who lived well into her nineties, I met only three times in rare family visits to the Old Country, and I can recall her in mere fleeting images, small and frail, always in a black cotton dress, the widow's shroud. Distance, culture, and language—all combined against us.

My mother's side lived near us in Kansas City, for a while just down the street, but they were equally distant. It was only when I was older that I learned much about them, and that while many of them blossomed with great promise in life, others nonetheless turned out to be terribly troubled.

In the 1990s, a cousin, Dick Jeck, became our family genealogist. He traced one branch of the clan on my mother's side—the Toelles— clear back to Germany and as far into the misty past as the early 1800s. Then he followed them forward, onto ships bound for New York and a settlement in Greenwich Village, then to a farm in eastern Wisconsin, about halfway between the booming industrial centers of Milwaukee and Chicago. There he focused on Henry B. Toelle, twenty years old in 1860, the oldest of fifteen children to a pair of German immigrants. He was born on March 27, 1840, in Greenwich Village.

Henry kept a five-year diary during the Civil War, and he documented almost every day of his young adult life during that period, even his most mundane chores. He milked cows and planted wheat. He husked corn and dug potatoes. When the hay got high, it had to be mowed. When the old barn leaked, he hammered nails. Even his afternoon thoughts he put down on paper—any idea that crossed his young, inquisitive mind walking to town and home again, or just to a neighbor's to visit or for music lessons.

6

Henry played the piano, the organ, and the melodeon. Sometimes he attended mass twice on Sundays, in the morning and then returning in the evening, once for the ritual, then back for the spiritual. He organized the church choir, and he encouraged the group into forming a club "for learning the art of singing," he wrote.

Like me, Henry also had a male relative who one day suddenly vanished. For him, it was an uncle, and he mentioned his loss on the opening pages of his diary. "My mother's father was a school teacher of the German Catholic public schools in Germany," he wrote. "My mother's brother was a glazier; he went on a journey to Rome and never was heard of since . . ."

For the years spanning the War between the States, Henry kept at his diary, rarely letting a night fall without recording some recollection of his day's adventures. But hardly a word did he devote to the Civil War or how the struggle was devastating the land.

He called his diary "The Life of Henry B. Toelle." Jeck sent me a copy, and I remember poring over the handwritten pages on a series of long nights, forgoing sleep to squint at the words often difficult to make out in the elegant flourish of Henry's penmanship.

He did mention a torchlight parade in Racine for Stephen A. Douglas, running against Abraham Lincoln in the 1860 presidential campaign. The Democratic candidate was speaking from a platform railcar when the train suddenly lurched forward and started to pull away. Quickly, Douglas cut short his remarks. He shouted, "The engine is the greatest pirate on earth! So I must leave you and bid you goodnight." The band played "Hail Columbia," and the cannons fired. "The people were very quiet," Henry wrote. "So that no disturbance took place."

Douglas lost, and the war came. A year into the conflict Henry described how he promised a friend and fellow musician that he would watch over some of his belongings while he went to fight for Mr. Lincoln: "Sept. 14th, 1861. Sat.—In Burlington . . . I saw military companies. . . . Had a conversation with E. Scherer. He gave me 'The Manual of Catholic Melodies' and the free use of his library and violin for the time till he will come back from war."

Henry himself was turned down for military service: "Sept. 2nd, 1862. Tues.—Was examined before Dr. Thompson if I was able to attend military duty. I was found unfit."

I thought to myself: here begins the first of my family misfits.

But I was wrong. Old Henry Toelle persevered. He made something of himself. He married Anna Mary Daniels of Brighton, Wisconsin, and they moved to Kansas City in 1869. Henry opened a German and English bookstore in the downtown area at 718 Main Street, just two blocks from what later became the city's skid row and the streets that swallowed up James Lyons. He served as a local agent for the Northwest Mutual Benevolent Association, out of Milwaukee. He played the organ at Sts. Peter and Paul Catholic Church. And he taught piano lessons. But as the thriving town at the marriage of two great rivers—the Missouri and the Kansas—began to sprawl and hoist itself over the big bluffs, Henry apparently felt that all the clatter and noise were too much for him. He saw the community growing too rapidly, too crowded and too pretentious for his small-town ways. He was a man who preferred plenty of breathing space, and insisted on fresh country air for his large family, much like he had enjoyed growing up on the Toelle family farm near Lake Michigan. Henry was content with a horse and a farm wagon; the streetcar was not for him.

So in 1882 he moved to Wea, a small Kansas farming community named after a local Native American tribe, and later a second farm outside a neighboring town called Paola. Now he felt more comfortable, more at home among the expanding German American families who were also abandoning the growing city. On Sundays the farmers and homesteaders gathered at a beautiful church in Wea, its Catholic steeple a beacon of faith above the fresh-plowed soil, the golden summer corn, the violet reflective sky. Henry continued to play the organ.

He also dabbled in local politics, and eventually got himself elected to the County Alliance and the Paola Township Board. He served on the Farmers Mutual Benefit Association and the Cemetery Board, too. He grew fat with age and a thick, dark beard framed his heavy jowls. In time the beard turned gray. In our family history he became almost Solomon-like, the patriarch filled with a heart so wise.

On his birthday in 1895, Henry was given an autographs book. It was quite the popular gift in its time, a fad mostly, and people enjoyed filling the pages with short rhymes and couplets from friends and loved ones. Sometimes you might write notes or a little verse to yourself, something to show others.

Henry used his book to once again chronicle his life. He signed the cover and underlined his name. He added his birth date in New

York City and his current rural address in Kansas. He also under-lined his age: "55 years old."

On page 7 he inscribed a small verse to his oldest girl, born in Kansas City in 1871:

> To my daughter, Frances,
> May peace and blessing be your lot
> And when I am dead for-get-me not.

He signed it simply, H. B. T.

Henry's wife and children adored him, but it was the church that was the center of town—both in Wea and in Paola. As the Wea com-munity grew, parishioners began building a new place of worship. They wanted a larger church and a higher steeple to reach closer to the heavens. The new structure opened its doors in 1895, but ten years later a heavy storm kicked up over the Kansas prairie and lightning struck the new steeple. The church fell. The farmers and the townspeople pulled together and set about building a replace-ment church, and just before it was completed a Kansas tornado whipped through Wea. The church fell again. So they rebuilt once more, and the new church was dedicated on May 29, 1906.

The Wea church, called Queen of the Holy Rosary, stands there today, a century old now, a testimony to the resolve of the Catho-lic faithful in rural Kansas. When home I often attend mass there, and the church history still recalls the grit of the old pioneer era. "Queen of the Holy Rosary was built and rebuilt three times with-in 11 years after a lightening [*sic*] strike and cyclone," the church bulletin reported. "The fortitude of our forefathers makes all of this possible."

Henry's second church in Paola, called Holy Trinity, also was born of hard times. One of the area's early priests, Father Ivo Schacht, was a horseback missionary, traveling a circuit in eastern Kansas to say mass at various communities, oftentimes in the homes of German and Irish immigrants. He eventually promised to build a church in Paola, but only if the parishioners could muster up the funds. He appointed a Frenchman named Fontaine Cartissiere to collect con-tributions from white settlers and Native Americans still camping in the area. "There was, however, a great disappointment in store for them," according to a history of Holy Trinity church.

When Father Schacht returned from one of his journeys, the Frenchman could not be found. He had run off with all of the donations. "Father Schacht was almost broken-hearted," the history reported. "He knew the sacrifice the people made to contribute the funds; he realized what additional burden it would be to give again." It turned out "the settlers were not daunted." All were in agreement: "They must have a church."

So Father Schacht went door-to-door himself. The church plates were filled once again, and an "old stone" structure was dedicated in 1860. But it would not last. By the time Henry Toelle was moving to the Paola area, Holy Trinity was fast falling apart. Large cracks had splintered the walls, and engineers concluded that the structure was no longer safe for services.

Like their friends in Wea, the Holy Trinity congregation began work on yet another church. It opened in 1880, made of sturdy brick with a bell tower, shingle roof, and plain glass windows. But it too was doomed. On the night of January 14, 1906, fire alarms jarred townspeople from sleep. Flames shot up through the shingles and out of the bell tower. In a few hours Holy Trinity was in ashes.

They rebuilt again. A third church drive was started, and Henry's son George Toelle joined a new select committee to solicit even more funds. Holy Trinity once more rose up, bricks and tower once again, and its cornerstone was laid May 27, 1906—just two days before the other new church was dedicated in Wea.

But Henry Toelle did not live to play the organ in either of the two new churches. In fact, he missed both dedications, in Wea and in Paola. In a cruel twist, Henry died of kidney failure on the very day that the stone was laid at Holy Trinity. He was sixty-six years old, a ripe old age in contrast to many of the males in my family. And although now he is gone, the twin churches and their two steeples remain. Indeed, there they stand today, proof that good men like Henry B. Toelle cannot be defeated and in death will not be forgotten, even in a family populated with male absconders.

Henry and Anna raised ten children in all. Their second to youngest was a little girl with golden hair and bright-pink cheeks. They named her Rose. She was my great-grandmother.

Rose moved to Kansas City and married a man from Texas named Thomas Norman. He worked as a waiter at the Kansas City Athletic Club and for the Morledge Fish & Oyster Company. They had two children. The first was my grandmother, Zillah, born in January 1915.

Then one regrettable day Thomas Norman up and vanished—another of my male lineage to clear the door, just as his son and namesake and his son-in-law too would both leave their families in the years ahead. But it was never certain why Rose's husband, my great-grandfather, left. One story had him telling Rose that he was stepping out for a pack of cigarettes. Be right back, he said. Another had him off on a grand tour of Chicago, and to take in the wonders of the World's Fair. Another version said he headed west to the Pacific and hired himself out on a line of cruise ships or a commercial steamer, nobody knew which, maybe both, waiting tables and working in the kitchen. From the portholes and on ports of call, he would see the world.

Really, it did not matter where he went. All that truly counted was that the old man was gone. Another male in my family had run off. This one did turn up eventually, however, when I was four years old and a telegram arrived in Kansas City telling us he was dead on the West Coast. They brought him back, and they buried him here at home, the home he had abandoned.

Rose raised the two children alone. She went to work as a phone operator at the National Bellas Hess clothing-catalog company, a multistory warehouse in the city's old rail yard and grain-elevator district, north of downtown. She rode the bus. But she did not give up her lust for life. That she had learned from her father, the indomitable Henry Toelle. Like him, she loved to sing and play the piano. She loved to dance. She especially loved to square dance. Like many of the women in our family line, deserted in marriage, trying to do the right thing, she turned her face to the world and put on a grand smile. Rose Toelle Norman showed great courage.

From this struggling home came my maternal grandmother, Zillah Rose Norman. Her name was taken from an ancient figure in the Old Testament, the second wife of a descendant of Cain, yet another male outcast. Translated from the Hebrew, her name means "shadow."

She was a brooding child. In almost every family photograph we have of the young girl she stares into the camera's eye and offers us little more than a thin grin. It was more a forced grin than anything else. Often she scowled. Really, the only photo of her smiling is that grainy one from November 1930, around the time of her wedding, with new husband James Lyons out in that field or backyard, wherever it was. She is not only smiling but bent over in joy.

Lord knows how she met James Lyons. But she must have loved the man. He was seven years older than she, and she was young, very young, and quite impressionable. Naive, too. So young that she lied on her marriage license application and declared she was eighteen years old. You had to be eighteen to marry in Missouri. Truth was, she was only fifteen. But she pulled that one off, somehow, and a Catholic priest married James and Zillah, and ten months after that my mother was born, Mary Elizabeth Lyons, the first of their two children.

They named my mother Mary after her father's mother, Mary Lyons, possibly, though my mother had no recollection of her any more than she knew her father. But she was blessed in other ways; my mother was born on September 8, and she shared her birthday with the Virgin Mary.

A second child, James Norman Lyons, came two years later, and by then, or maybe even before then, my grandfather was gone. They divorced.

Zillah next married a fellow named James Jameson. Little survives to tell of him. Oh, yes, he left, too. I am probably not even spelling his name right, suspecting his first name, James, is just a nickname for his last. Old city directories spell it several different ways, and said he worked as a stonemason. Some in the family used to say he walked with a limp. But limp or no limp, walk he did. He went right out the door, and he never came back, was never heard from again.

Zillah married for a third time; this man's name was Melvin Ralph Stark. Unfortunately, he stuck around. He was a brute of a man, a horrific drunk, a deeply bitter racist. When pressed, my mother would tell terrible stories about her stepfather—he climbed out back windows when police knocked at the front, and as a teenager she was sent to the corner tavern to fetch him home. During my childhood we lived just a block from their house but were strictly forbidden to visit.

Once my best friend, Dave Nesbitt, and I were breaking soda bottles over rocks—what boy in the 1950s could not pass hours throwing rocks and bottles on a hotter-than-blazes summer afternoon? We were in a vacant lot behind a small grocery, about halfway between my home and where my grandmother lived. Stupidly, I sliced my finger on the broken glass, and when the blood would not stop, we panicked about having to tell my parents.

Dave came up with a keen idea. "Why not go to your grandma's?" he suggested.

To Zillah's we went, and while she bandaged the finger—a rather deep cut, I still carry the scar—she also phoned my mother, and that night I was scolded and grounded, not for throwing rocks and not for breaking bottles but for committing a more unpardonable sin. I had gone to that house.

We saw them rarely—a Christmas here, a Thanksgiving there, sadly memorable for the old man's rages. Once Stark swung a hoe at my father; another time he reached for a pistol. Often after Sunday mass we could hear him tossing obscenities from his car in front of the church, ordering us to hurry our grandmother out. I can hear him screaming still, threatening to kill me. At last he died in the mid-1970s, his booze-rotten liver bloated and burst. Outside our immediate family no one showed up for his funeral, except two nephews we never knew he had.

Poor old Grandma Zillah, the shadowy one: she made poor choices in men. And of her first husband, the one who fathered my mother, the first to get away, she never spoke. So as a boy I had to imagine a grandfather, to dream one up. He had to be strong and brave, like a superhero in today's fantasy world. I built mine around my real grandfather James Lyons, the mystery figure no one could explain to us—except that he had died a prisoner. In my head I saw him as a sort of Count of Monte Cristo, the grand romantic who wrapped himself in a dead man's blanket and was flung from the prison tower.

Other boys on the school playground could brag about grandfathers who took them fishing and to ball games, or off for a drive in fast cars. Childhood rivalry can be a terrible thing, and my friend Dave Nesbitt had me beat by a mile. His grandfather was none other than Lt. Harry D. Nesbitt.

By the 1950s, when we were growing up, the legendary Lieutenant Nesbitt was already a high-ranking Kansas City police official. He had reached that vaunted status through an incredible string of brave encounters and shoot-'em-ups with bad guys, begun after he first donned a patrolman's cap in May 1929 in the old Westport precinct. Even in his retirement, reflecting back on his police exploits, Lieutenant Nesbitt was pictured in the *Kansas City Star* with his hat cocked on his head, his revolver in his hand, his fingers coolly cradling the handgun. He played the part perfectly, and oh, boy, did the newspapers love police officer Harry Nesbitt. They dubbed him the "straight-shooting detective." They praised him for his quick draw and his "unerring aim." He seemed on duty day and night, twiddling the buttons on his police scanner at home and chasing crooks on the way to work and back. Harry Nesbitt, the papers solemnly reported, was "aggressive." He had, the papers said, "engaged in many gun battles and has killed several bandits."

Yes, my pal Dave Nesbitt had me clobbered in the grandfather department. Or so it seemed.

In 1931 Harry Nesbitt and his partner unarmed a first-time bandit who robbed a young lady named Miss Ruby Love. The bandit, Robert Wilcox Terry, was actually a twenty-eight-year-old feed salesman from Des Moines. He lost his job and left his wife and children. He came to Kansas City, found work at a local mill, and lost that job inside of two weeks. Now he was desperate. So desperate that he was down to his last dime.

Terry bought a toy cap pistol with that ten cents. He climbed into his old model Chrysler and began cruising the streets. He spotted Miss Love and robbed her of fifty-two cents. He took her hundred-dollar ring, too.

Nesbitt and his partner heard the report of the robbery and within minutes overtook the Chrysler. Fast-thinking Harry Nesbitt arrested Terry with the ring and the fifty-two cents still fresh in his pockets. It meant a letter of commendation, noting that Terry's arrest was the seventh bandit Nesbitt had nabbed in the past two nights. Officer Harry Nesbitt was off and running.

In 1936 he and another partner killed an auto thief after a wild police chase through Kansas City. Nesbitt pushed the siren button as they pursued H. Frank Cordell, a twenty-seven-year-old former truck driver. He fired warning shots into the air for seven blocks, chasing the thief at dizzying speeds. When Cordell made a sharp turn, Nesbitt fired into the back of the stolen vehicle. When the chase ended, Cordell was slumped over the wheel, a bullet to the back of the neck.

More promotions came Nesbitt's way. He won awards, sometimes twenty-five or fifty dollars at a pop, then a princely sum for a street cop with a young family.

And Dead-Eye Harry Nesbitt kept at it. He shot two men for kidnapping taxi drivers. He chased a car stolen by the notorious Matthew (Beans) Bechina until Bechina crashed it into a tree. Bechina hit the tree after Nesbitt fired and grazed him in the ear. He shot and killed Thomas J. Jones, who was suspected of beating and choking women after robbing them.

Another time Nesbitt and two fellow cops went after a desperado holed up in a rooming house east of downtown. The man would not come out, so Nesbitt decided to go in. "Come on, boys," he signaled. "Let's go!"

One of the cops kicked in the door, and he was shot and wounded. Another was hit in the arm. Unnerved, undaunted, Nesbitt rose up and fired five times. When the gun smoke cleared, Nesbitt was still standing. The desperado was dead on the floor.

They held a ceremony at City Hall, and Nesbitt collected an eighty-dollar award. "I'm not giving you this check for killing men," city manager H. F. McElroy told him. "But for doing your duty in a most courageous manner." The city manager added, with a chuckle, "Get your men alive, when possible."

Nesbitt let out a big grin.

By 1949, the year after my grandfather died in the city jail, Dave Nesbitt's grandfather won the biggest prize of all. He was promoted to head of the Kansas City police homicide unit. In all, he had worked as a city cop for just short of four decades, and when he retired, he shrugged and said, "Well, I think thirty-nine years as a police officer is long enough."

So this was what I was faced with during grade school recess or playing around the old neighborhood. I just knew that to survive I had to go the other boys' stories one better. I did not have any facts to know what had really happened to my grandfather, what he was really all about, but I sure had no problem making them up. And I was not going to let Dave Nesbitt and his pistol-packing grandfather or anyone else take me lying down.

I decided: who wants to be Marshal Dillon when you can be Jesse James? My grandfather, I began to boast, was a criminal. Oh, yeah, he was a real-life bad guy. Better yet, he went to jail!

Wild ideas, they were. Maybe my grandfather never died in prison after all. Maybe he scaled the prison wall one moonlit night and outran the guards with guns ablaze and bloodhounds at the leash.

Sometimes unable to sleep in the wood-paneled bedroom I shared with two younger brothers, the electric fan slowly turning in the summer dusk, my imagination whisked me down dusty roads and into the big cities, the cops chasing me and old Granddad as we lived it up high on the lam. Or I pictured coming home from school some afternoon and finding him in the living room, sitting right there in his Monte Cristo glory, ready to thrill us with wide-eyed stories about bullets and bandits. I bet he'd show me a prison tattoo.

But James Lyons never turned up. He never took me on any daring rides. I went on to high school, and he melted into the back of my mind, way, way back there. Then the summer after graduation I worked as a delivery boy for the Kansas City Police Department, driving around town in the days before faxes and e-mail to pick up police reports and deliver them to headquarters downtown. One of the stops I remember most was the Canine Unit, where the police dogs were kept. I recall it not for the dogs but because the kennels were located next to the Municipal Farm, up a narrow, winding road and atop a high hill. From the kennels I could see the jail's bone-white walls, and I'd pause and think, "So here is the place."

Driving back down I wondered how different things might have been had life not taken its unexplainable turns, and I thought that death soon enough comes for us all. Watching the jail receding in my rearview mirror I was left to wonder how my grandfather met his.

Still, I tucked such thoughts away. I went on to a newspaper career. I married and raised my own family. I moved to Washington and California and back to Washington. Yet once or twice, when I returned home for visits, we would talk about family matters, and my mother might bring it up again, quite gingerly, "If only we knew . . ."

But I did not want to know. Not then. Not for the longest time. As an adult, with three sons of my own, I felt having a prisoner for a grandfather was no longer glorious; it was shameful, some kind of black mark. Peeling back the family onion would produce only tears. Life is filled with difficulties enough; why dig for more?

And Mom was nearing the end of her life. She had been long ago diagnosed with multiple sclerosis, and we had watched her decline—a cane, a wheelchair, a hospital bed at home. Then she, too, was gone. And when I thought of James Lyons, if I thought of him at all, it was not out of any real curiosity or for a genealogical hobby, so popular today. It was not out of any intrigue from television shows about cold-case mysteries or crime-scene investigations. My approach was born out of pure guilt. If I was going to track him down, I should have started years earlier. Now I am in my midfifties, but ten or twenty years ago I might have found someone still alive or at least with memories intact, guards or inmates, maybe the county coroner or the chief of detectives. Some documents or other paperwork might not have been long ago trucked out to the city landfill.

The Jackson County coroner in 1948, for instance, was an elected position, and when he left office he routinely took his files home. The coroner then was a man named Walker; he is dead, and his grandson had no idea whatever became of his autopsy reports. Then I discovered that Walker was not a pathologist and that the actual postmortem on my grandfather was performed by a doctor named Upsher, and that when he retired he turned his records over to a local hospital. But Upsher is long dead, too, and the hospital, where my first son was born, two months premature, has since been torn down to make room for a federal government high-rise. Gone with it are the pathologist's records.

I e-mailed the office at the cemetery; you can't tear down a cemetery. Sharon Vallejo responded.

"Good morning, Richard," she e-mailed me. "What I found is probably not much more than you already have. I have in my records that James P. Lyons was buried in Mt. Calvary KCK 5-28-1948. His burial location is Section 3 Old Lot 147 Space 9. I do show Butler being the Funeral home. I have that he passed by way of a broken neck. I am so sorry that I do not have anything else than this." She added, "Thanks for inquiring."

Any kind of documents detailing my grandfather's arrest, conviction, and death were difficult to locate, many committed to dust years ago. Back then still-open homicide investigations were to be turned over to the clerk of the county court, then an elected position, too. That post is now held by an appointee, and she had no clue where something sixty years old might be. Nor did she have any interest in finding out.

Other county officials were much more helpful, especially the county attorney. He directed me out to the limestone caves along the Missouri River where government records are stored. There I unearthed grand jury reports about substandard jail conditions and a smattering of old criminal cases from 1948. But not a word about

James Lyons was crammed inside those frayed cardboard boxes. No mention of a jailhouse murder, either.

Equally frustrating was the rush to find someone still alive, anyone old enough to tell. In census records from 1930 I noticed that a Mary D. Burris, then eight years old, was living with my grandfather at the Lyons family home. I guessed she was his niece, and I figured she would have been twenty-six when her uncle, my grandfather, died. She would have known what happened. But how do I find Mary D. Burris?

Several months went by before I came across letters written by my grandfather's brother to a sister named Anna Burris. Through obituaries I realized she later became Anna Graham, and on a hunch I called the family cemetery and sure enough they had Anna Graham. She had died in 1989, and her obit listed just one daughter, a Dee Millstead. Was this Mary D. Burris?

I started calling the Millsteads in the phone book, and the second one turned out to have been Dee Millstead's sister-in-law. The woman said she and Mary D. Burris, who always went by her middle initial, had married Millstead brothers. She remembered my grandfather's sister Anna Graham, too. She dismissed her as an obnoxious Irish drunk who married five times and ended up living alone in an apartment in the center city. But it was Dee Millstead that I was desperate to find. Well, said the sister-in-law, that's the right one. She was born Mary D. Burris but everyone called her Dee, and then she married a Millstead.

Yes, yes, that's the one, I told the woman. I'm looking for his wife, Dee Millstead, born Mary D. Burris.

Well, you just missed her, the woman told me. She died two years ago.

Eventually, I located her daughter, Pat Theno. A beautiful woman, she invited me into her suburban home near the Kansas City International Airport. We opened up cartons of photographs of her mother and grandmother—and the great-grandmother from Ireland the two of us shared.

Pat said her grandmother Anna Lyons Graham, my grandfather's sister, had indeed been married five times, though to be fair, she pointed out that the last two marriages were to the same man. In her later years Anna lived alone on Jackson Street, spending nights, days too, a half block down the street at a country-western bar called the

Jackson Hole. She loved to dance and sing; she laughed and called herself a "floozy." But she did not keep returning to that bar for the honky-tonk; it was the whiskey that summoned her. She died alone, the last of the Lyons family.

Yet what of my grandfather? I asked.

Pat would have been eight years old when he died; maybe she knew something. Maybe she was told what had happened. Maybe the truth was in her, if what the adults had told her was the truth.

"I remember Grandma talking about a brother named Jimmy," Pat told me. "Other than that he drank a lot, I don't know. They said he was drinking and that he fell and hit his head, accidentally."

Another woman I met turned out to be another soul mate. Her name is Gloria Lundy. She is a nurse and amateur genealogist and lives with her husband and four large dogs in Gladstone, Missouri, another suburb not far from the airport. We met at her house, and I told her how I thought my grandfather had died.

Immediately, she was suspicious. "Solitary confinement?" she said. "Hmm. I wonder how that happened."

She told me her story. She also had stumbled on the Missouri death records on the Internet and typed in the name of her grandfather Robert Jones Sr. He had left their family long ago, too, and though not an alcoholic, he died penniless in 1929 from complications from diabetes at the city's General Hospital. What surprised her was that he was buried at the old potter's cemetery next to the Kansas City Municipal Farm. That launched her on a drive to record the names of all the paupers who were buried there, some five thousand men, women, and children, and to preserve the area as hallowed ground. Sometimes she goes out there and brings home rusted metal staves and other markings from the old grave sites. She packs them in boxes, and the boxes she stacks up in her garage.

So like me, although not proud of her grandfather either, she sought some measure of closure in knowing who he was, and what he had become.

"I started crying," she told me over her breakfast table one day. "I had finally found something about him, the first tangible evidence I'd found of my grandfather. I finally felt connected to him."

In my case, when city and county officials could not locate documents about my grandfather, I began asking for information about his one brother. Joseph P. Lyons Jr. had his problems with the bottle, too, and his troubles with the law. With my brother Jeff along, I returned to the limestone caves, hunting this time for anything about Joseph Lyons's arrest, in November 1936.

We stared up at shelves twelve feet high, stacked with heavy, hard-bound ledger books, one for each Jackson County circuit judge for each year. Climbing atop a steel ladder, I lowered them down to my brother, one after another, and we heaved them onto a metal table and began thumbing through the pages. A half-dozen ledgers, a dozen, and finally we landed inside the docket book for Jackson County judge Albert A. Ridge, a longtime friend and political ally of future president Harry Truman, and the November court term of 1936. There our eyes stopped at this notation: *State of Missouri v. Joseph P. Lyons,* who pleads guilty to grand larceny and is sentenced to three years in prison.

The clerks in the caves rushed around the corner and caught us covered in dust from the old leather binders, our fingers cut from turning the still-crisp pages. We were giggling and high-fiving, and making quite the nuisance, and now we wanted to see the actual court papers. They directed us to more boxes in stacks marked for disposal, and since we now had a docket number, C-17334, we found them, too, including the formal charges that said Joseph Patrick Lyons Jr. was a thief and had stolen from the hospital where he and my grandfather worked as janitors.

Now let me see the prosecution files, I said.

Impossible, the clerks answered. Anything from the prosecutor's office that was "prewar"—World War II, they meant—had been long ago destroyed.

Show me.

So they led us to another alcove in the caves and to more tall shelves and more stacks of undated brown boxes, hundreds, it seemed. But they warned us that none went back far enough.

I insisted we open the first box.

Have at it, they shrugged.

The oldest carton had material from 1929, and soon we were laughing and clapping again and flying through these boxes, too, realizing that each one contained a month's worth of prosecutor's files. We tore through them, 1931 and 1934 and higher still, our shirts dirtier and our fingers bleeding from more paper cuts, and then I flipped through the file folders in the box I found for November 1936. To a great hurrah I lifted out my uncle's records.

Inside was his signed confession, written in blue ink, the signature shaky but the name still clearly legible after almost three-quarters of a century being buried in a box stored under the earth.

"I have never been in any trouble to speak of," my grandfather's brother told the police, "with the exception of being arrested several times for being drunk."

That evening we went out for Chinese. I ordered the chicken with mixed vegetables, and a glass of Sapporo. I was thinking what a re-markable day it had been for a treasure hunt. At the end of the meal they brought fortune cookies. Mine hit home: "Cleaning up the past will always clear up the future."

It seemed I kept bumping into my grandfather in the present, too, in the most unlikely of places, as if he were trying to reach out to me, to introduce me to his life and how he had lived it, perhaps to apologize, if he had that in him.

He touched me in the subtlest of ways. Once after an evening·mass the pastor, himself an Irish immigrant, invited a group of us to the rectory for a Christmas reception. He brought out a tray of spir-its, and I tried to beg off. The hardest liquor I had ever had was draft beer, and in my youth plenty of that. But the priest insisted I sample his Irish whiskeys, and I was pleasantly surprised at how smooth it went down. Maybe twice a week now—okay, sometimes more—I pour a shot glass of Bushmills, neat, without ice.

At work I often encountered the homeless in downtown Wash-ington. I had my own rule of giving pocket change or a dollar to any woman or child who sought my aid. The men I passed briskly by; are there no workhouses? But now I watched the men closely, and when they stretched out a gnarled hand or jangled a paper cup, I sometimes stopped and leaned down. I looked beyond the thick beards and the soiled, matted hair, past the hot stench of their breath and the rotted teeth. I peered deeply into their sunken eyes. In there too I was searching for my grandfather. And when I realized I had gotten too close I placed a quarter or a folded dollar into their open palm. Put it toward lunch, I would say, pointing to a sandwich shop across the street. But I always knew where the money went. Food may fill the body, but drink nourishes the soul.

On one trip back to Kansas City I made a driving tour of the various spots where my grandfather had lived, hoping to maybe get inside his shoes after he had walked out on my grandmother. I ended up where he ended up, at Fifth and Main streets, in his day the town's skid row, today nothing more than a half-vacant block cut off by an interstate highway. I stepped out of the rental car, and while I listened, I could not hear. Gone was the din of barroom clatter, of derelicts snoring in the bushes, of bums collapsing on the sidewalk. All was quiet now, the parade and the pain over, and I was left straining for the long-ago echo of the whack of the policeman's baton. "Move along, pal. Move along." But only the whir of the cars on the freeway reached me, speeding to get past this place.

Yet I was here, and I was going to find him. So I believed, just like I had as a boy, that we were destined to meet after all. Once he lived large in my imagination. Now I wanted to follow his footsteps, to hunt the old man down.

As I plodded on, he never left my thoughts. I am a great walker; I have walked for an hour almost every morning for the past dozen years, down neighborhood trails or in big cities or strange small communities, whether at home or in my travels for work. Sometimes in the summer when the light lasts, I walk a second hour.

James Lyons often enters my mind during these solitary journeys, and what was funny was that along the way to find him I learned about two other famous walkers. One was named Potee, and he used to prance up and down Main Street in overcoat and hat. He twirled a cane in the heart of Kansas City when it was first being carved up out of the Missouri River bluffs. The other was the scraggly Irishman named McRill who hailed himself the "Walking Marvel." He covered the same streets as Potee, but years later, when it was an all but abandoned and bolted-up neighborhood and had become the city's skid row, he and my grandfather shared the same flophouse.

Yet in all my walks, my treasure hunts in caves for city and county records, even a trip to the Municipal Farm one chilly winter day, I never expected anyone to be arrested or sent to prison for a sixty-year-old suspicious dead body. No, but I did come to appreciate that the family history that unfolds before we are born no matter how dark or how painful still needs to be known. And that regardless of how awful it might have been, we endure. And that even if it is too late to correct an old injustice, it does not mean that the crime should go forever unmentioned. We summon our strength from the things that remain.

So I kept searching, hoping that when the day came and I was done, however things wound up, I could give my mother in heaven something she long had wanted on earth—the gift of her past.

CHAPTER 3

I started with his death certificate. It listed my grandfather's parents as Joseph P. Lyons and Mary Connors and noted that they had emigrated from Ireland. He had come from Belfast to America in 1893, and settled in Kansas City, Kansas, five years later. I also found a ship manifest from the *Britannic*, in its day the fastest sail on the Atlantic. One September day the ship entered New York Harbor, and a young woman named Mary Connors, a "housemaid" carrying a bag of luggage in each hand, stepped off at Ellis Island.

From the immigration records I traced her journey. Old census tracts placed her in the Kansas City area just before the turn of the century. City directories at the Kansas City Public Library chronicled her marriage and growing family. The Library of Congress in Washington, a subway ride from my home, had a microfilm roll of the May 1948 *Kansas City Star* newspaper. There I found my grandfather's obituary. Now I had the names of his three surviving sisters. Tapping into the computerized Social Security Index and other Internet resources, I found when they died and went back to Capitol Hill and the microfilm machine, and printed out their obituaries, too. That took me to their grandchildren—my cousins.

I phoned them, feeling a bit like the outcast orphan, awkwardly approaching unknown relatives for the first time, summoning the courage to seek their help. But after thirty-five years as a reporter in the newspaper business I had hardened to the practice of cold-calling people for information, and they were kind and supportive and began filling in some family details. But they knew very little, really, about their ancestors. And they knew nothing at all about my grandfather or what had happened to him, and certainly nothing about any prison.

So I went looking for myself. I learned that Mary Connors settled in Kansas City, Kansas, and there at St. Mary's Church in October

1899 married Joseph Lyons. A microfilm copy of the *Kansas City (Kans.) Gazette* for October 25, 1899, reported that Joseph Lyons and Mariah Connors were among four couples issued marriage licenses by Judge Kimble P. Snyder.

Judge Snyder came from a farm in southeastern Illinois, and he had served in the Civil War, at fourteen the youngest soldier in his Yankee regiment. He moved here in 1888, and took up positions as city attorney and city counselor. People always thought him honest and fair, and quick with a smile, a handshake, and a kind word. He was fresh on the bench when he granted the marriage license to Joseph and Mary.

I flipped through the rest of the pages of the *Gazette* for that day, and the day before, and the following day as well, the whole week eventually, trying to get a feel for how life was lived in their community on the Kansas side of the metropolis at that time, right on the edge of a new century. I came away surprised that many of the news items concerned issues that would haunt the young Lyons family in the years ahead. Though the incidents did not directly touch on the family then, many of them in the coming years would scar them deeply.

The curse of alcoholism that would ruin many in the Lyons family hovered over the Kansas City, Kansas, community—a boiling pot of immigrants from the British Isles and eastern Europe. A coroner's jury ruled that three men, Mike Zunie, John Perodinac, and George Muhar, "must stand trial" for the slaying of an Austrian immigrant named John Yarnavic. He was killed in a drunken row in a Kansas River saloon on James Street two weeks earlier, beaten to death with a beer glass. Booze bred violence, and that brought more trouble.

A pair of boxcar thieves named John Ryan and George Anderson were arrested and fined one hundred dollars each. Police added an additional charge of vagrancy. Officials sent them to "the rock pile."

An Irish fellow named "Red" Murphy showed up. He was notorious in "all of the large cities in the West as a dangerous crook and confidence man." Red was plucked up off the street in Kansas City, Kansas, and alone behind closed doors police gave him a "sweating." They gave him something else too: fifteen minutes to leave town.

Divorce and child abandonment were wrecking families, the rich and the poor alike. Charles E. Lobdell, who had formerly worked for the *Wyandotte (Kans.) Tribune,* sued his wife for divorce. He alleged abandonment. But Mrs. Lobdell hit him back, announcing that she would not be so summarily discarded. She said she would fight him for alimony.

Labor in the railroads, the stockyards, and the meatpacking houses, where Joseph Lyons supported his family and where my grandfather briefly followed, could be backbreaking, dangerous places to toil. The river bottoms were filled with cattle, hog, and sheep pens, and this week one of the sheep pen buildings burned to the ground, further fouling the air.

Death or injury on the job could be swift, typically without warning. George Fuller was struck by a falling block in the Santa Fe yards; it broke his collar bone. With Fuller out of work, his family would suffer. Other times tempers flared in the stench of the packing plants. John F. Beilstein, a butcher, shot and killed Edward Clark at the Armour plant. He was arraigned and held without bail.

Illness and disease ran rampant in a community boxed in by the brace of two mighty rivers and up against the insect-filled stock pens and packing plants.

The Lyons family would be tested by the flu and meningitis. The scourge of tuberculosis often shadowed their door. When they opened their daily newspaper, their eyes would stop at the ads offering miracle cures.

A Dr. Mendel from the French Academy of Medicine claimed to have "thus far treated" sixteen tuberculosis patients and two others suffering from bronchitis. A mere week or two could do the trick, enough to stop the coughing and hacking and expectoration. Soon enough, he proclaimed, your son would happily return to his good old self, and a new life filled with "sleep, appetite and strength."

The fears of the poor were real, and the fear of death most of all. Philip Young was a "little boy" living in the Soldiers' Orphans' home at Atchison, Kansas. It actually was a juvenile detention facility, and one night Philip sneaked out and headed south. He walked all the way to Kansas City, Kansas, a trip by foot of more than forty miles. But Philip was determined to get there; his mother lay dying in Kansas City, Kansas. He made it in time; he saw his mother and she died, and then he was returned to the home in Atchison. Soon enough he escaped again, though, and now "the police are looking for him."

The young Lyons family was equally poor, equally desperate and suffering. In all Joseph and Mary had seven children, and my grandfather, the next to last, was named for his grandfather in Ireland, James Lyons. The couple had followed two waves of famine Irish to America. Twenty years before Joseph and Mary landed, Irish immigrants already made up a fifth of the community's unskilled labor force. They helped carve a bistate metropolis from a sprawl of packinghouses and cattle and rail-switching yards. They built homes and filled churches. And they stocked the Irish saloons.

On the Kansas City, Missouri, side lived another son of Irish immigrants named Pendergast—Boss Tom to all in the city. His brothers kept a saloon in the old district at 508 Main Street, and he saw to it that the bars and the nightclubs in Kansas City stayed open and the police stayed away. He ran companies that wholesaled liquor and readily mixed concrete, and his cement paved Tom's town. The Jackson County Democratic Club served as his base of operations, and there long lines formed outside and up the stairs to his second-floor office, especially crowded during those long years of the Great Depression. He personally doled out city contracts and chose the politicians. He provided jobs for the newly arrived and free meals to the newly unemployed. He kept office hours at the club at 1908 Main Street and went home to a three-story mansion on the city's most fashionable thoroughfare, Ward Parkway. Pendergast made bundles of money, lost bundles at the racetrack, and was bundled off to prison for tax evasion. The vice president of the United States, his loyal pal Harry Truman, attended his funeral.

Pendergast died in 1945, three years before my grandfather, and the nation's press took careful note of his passing. The *Saturday Evening Post* that year proclaimed that while the boss might be gone, his regime carried on, particularly in its "control" over Jackson County politics, and it was those county politics that ran the sheriff's office that was assigned to investigate my grandfather's death. Kansas City was the "crossroads of America," said the magazine, and Pendergast's death launched a traumatic crossroads period for the city itself.

"Pendergast was smart, decisive and full of the qualities of command and leadership," reported the *Saturday Evening Post*. "He could stuff a ballot box as deftly as a Midwest farm wife can stuff a hen . . . He went to mass every morning and then went to his office, from where he ran Kansas City just as wide open as she would run, and the idea of conflict between his professed moral beliefs and his actions never seemed to enter his head. There were crap games in every pool hall and bookie joint. Whiskey was always fifty cents more a bottle in Kansas City. . . ."

Tom Pendergast was dead, but the power he forged in life lived on. He hired the jail guards, and he hired the homicide detectives, and they continued to operate well after his funeral. Truman returned to Washington and soon became president of the United States, and back in Kansas City the boss's influence continued undiminished in the middle of the country—even as my grandfather was taken to that jail.

In this twin border-state community, the two Kansas Cities where fortunes were won and lost and won again—sometimes—Joseph P. Lyons Sr. lifted himself up into a solid man. He worked long days in the Kansas City rail yards and at the giant packing centers—huge industries along the Missouri and Kansas river bottoms, rival only to the slaughterhouses in Chicago. For a while he toiled as a scaler at a cold-storage plant, weighing the hoary, bloody carcasses before they were butchered, wrapped, and shipped out. His family growing, he tried to make his way out of the muck of the packinghouses and for a while took a white-collar job in sales. But by 1908, the year James was born, he needed more reliable employment. Soon he was back on the killing floor.

For forty-four years he lived in Kansas City, Kansas. He became one of the oldest members of the Holy Name Society of St. Thomas Church at Pyle Street and Shawnee Avenue in the Armourdale district of Kansas City, Kansas—a low-lying section of Kansas River bottomland. It was named after one of the largest meatpacking companies around. For four decades he attended mass there. From St. Thomas too he was buried, just before the spring of 1942. He was sixty-eight.

Pat Theno gave me two photographs of our great-grandfather. They were taken near the end of his life. He is seated in a chair on a lawn, his wife, Mary, standing at his left, his daughter Anna at his right. He is bald but still broad shouldered and still wearing his long-sleeved work shirt, buttoned at the collar. Like his son James and me as well, he has thin eyes and a thin mouth. In the second photograph he is cradling a little girl on his lap, perhaps Pat. We are unsure. But the old man is smiling, almost wanting to burst with pride.

Mary lived long enough to bury her husband and four of their seven children. The young woman full of promise grew old with the century, a mother and a grandmother and a great-grandmother, gray and in the end broken of heart. Another cousin showed me a black-and-white photograph, date unknown but most likely in the early 1950s. She stands on a porch, with thin, wispy white hair, a blustery apron about her waist. A broom leans against the wall, as though she has paused briefly for the picture. She is smiling, that same narrow, thin smile. She does not seem happy.

"She had one drink a year," said Ronald Seufert, one of the older Lyons cousins able to briefly recall the family matriarch. "Eggnog and Irish whiskey on Christmas Eve. One of my uncles was the supplier of the whiskey. My father got the eggnog."

Another cousin, Rick Neumann, who at my age cannot remember her at all, said she apparently enjoyed more than just a Christmas toast. "They remembered Great-Grandma Lyons carried a bottle with her. She was a whiskey drinker, and Dad always told me how Great-Grandma Lyons drank."

Another cousin, Donna Rohner, said, "My dad loved her dearly. He loved the old woman to pieces. She didn't want anybody to know her age, and they had to go to Ireland to find out how old she was when she died. That's why it's wrong on her grave marker. Her last address was Belfast, and she kept this old Catholic book, *Rules to Live By*, with these arcane rules from the Old Country, like cows are worth more than a wife. . . . She'd wait for my dad to come home when she lived with us on Fourteenth Street. On St. Patrick's Day they'd load into the car, and she had all these Irish taverns she just had to visit. She only drank Irish whiskey. She was five feet tall, and she could outdrink anybody, my dad said."

Her grief ran deep.

She sent her children to St. Thomas, a brown-brick Catholic church and school that, though today boarded up, still serves as a community lighthouse, its steeple and bell tower jutting above the Kansas City, Kansas, skyline. The parish was begun in 1883, just before Joseph and Mary arrived, and a new church building was completed in 1919, just at the end of the First World War. Like those churches in rural Kansas where Henry Toelle worshiped, St. Thomas also had to be rebuilt after its own natural disaster. This one was the Kansas City, Kansas, flood of 1903. Even the church basement took in high water and was washed out. So parishioners cleaned out the basement and started attending mass down below while another new church was being constructed above them.

The pastor was Rev. John P. McKenna, as good an Irish-sounding name as any. He was born in Iona, Prince Edward Island, Canada, and the white-haired priest, just thirty years old, came to St. Thomas in 1914. Services were still being held in the basement then, with some four hundred families crammed in below while workers above kept hammering and nailing and laying the new brown bricks. When the construction was finished the parishioners came up into the sunshine and the splendor of their new church. In time the rains would return.

For now, Joseph and Mary Lyons had their children baptized at St. Thomas; my grandfather would have been baptized in the basement. There also they attended funeral masses for Mary's husband and four of her children. My grandfather's funeral in 1948 was held in the new church building aboveground.

Mary and Joseph's third child, Sarah, died in 1904 of meningitis; she was just sixteen months old. Alice Irene, the youngest of their seven children, came down with the dreaded influenza. They lost her in 1918; she was eight. In March 1942 Mary's husband, Joseph, died, and two months later went her oldest son, thirty-five-year-old Joseph Jr. Tuberculosis carried him away.

I found the newspaper obituary for Joseph Jr. and was immediately struck by the sentence that claimed he died at home. That could not be right; nobody died at home with tuberculosis, a highly contagious disease. So I wrote to the Kansas state capital in Topeka for his death certificate, and when it arrived some weeks later, it floored me. He did not die at home at all. He died in the Kansas State Penitentiary (KSP) at Lansing. Poor Mary Lyons lost both her sons to prison.

I phoned Lansing, but an aide in the warden's office, Brett Peterson, doubted they would have much on a prisoner from so many years ago. He promised to check, though, and said he would call back. Later that day, quite amazed, Peterson told me that clerks in the prison records office located an old box and pulled it off the shelf. Dusting off the top and flipping through the box they found inside a worn index card. Peterson faxed me a copy. It said:

No. 6982
Name: Lyons, Joseph
Alias: Joseph P. Lyons
Crime: Larceny from Dwelling
Term: 1–7 Yrs.
Rec.: 10-27-39
From: Wyandotte
Race: White

At the bottom of the card, for information about the prisoner's discharge, there was no date recorded. Instead, handwritten, was this notation: "Discharge: Died 5-18-42."

The curtain rose on my uncle's life of crime—such as it was—in March 1932, when he drew thirty days in the Kansas City, Kansas, city jail "for being drunk." I reviewed his Kansas prison records at the state historical society in Topeka. I found another prison jacket for him at the Missouri state capital in Jefferson City, and then records from a third incarceration back again in Kansas. Joseph P. Lyons Jr. had been a very, very busy man.

Born in 1906, he was two years older than my grandfather. He never married, while my grandfather went to the altar at least four times that I could find. Joseph died a single man, and a petty crook, a triple failure, not counting that first thirty days in the city jail. Not much of a role model for his younger brother. Except maybe in one way the brothers were quite compatible: both were prisoners of the bottle.

One thing more: Joseph first went to state prison in late 1933, right around the time that my grandfather would have been leaving my grandmother.

Joseph was arrested in November 1933 for burglarizing the home of the Lyons family's next-door neighbor in Kansas City, Kansas. He broke into the house of Mr. and Mrs. James Pappas and started scooping up anything in reach. He stole a .32-caliber Colt revolver, a gold chain and diamond necklace, a black leatherette sheepskin coat, fifty pieces of Rogers silver, nineteen knives, and thirty-one forks. He even shook loose $7.00 in dimes from a small piggy bank. His total take was valued at $143.50.

The records do not tell how they caught him, but I can assume the Pappas family was none too happy when they came home and discovered the broken window. I can only guess they probably knew their neighbors, too. With Joseph unable to make a $1,500 bond, the sheriff locked him up in the Wyandotte County Jail in Kansas City, Kansas. Prosecutors charged him with burglary and grand larceny, and he was bound over for trial.

The case never got that far. In January 1934 he pleaded guilty, and the judge sentenced him, according to the records, "to state Penitentiary for a term of not exceeding five years at hard labor." They drove him out to Lansing, but first they waited a few days. There had been a spectacular prison break on the day after Joseph was sentenced. Seven desperadoes went over the wall on a makeshift ladder—burglars, bank robbers, even a murderer; they all split up. Two of them kidnapped a teacher. A year earlier eleven prisoners had broken free through a tower gate. That time they kidnapped the warden himself, and two of his guards. Even a gun battle could not stop them.

Lansing at that time was not exactly like Kansas City's Municipal Farm. The Kansas inmates were clearly more hardened criminals, sentenced for much more grievous offenses. But prison is prison, and in Lansing the escapees, those who were caught and not killed, said afterward that they fled the penitentiary because they hated the conditions there. Mostly what they hated were trips to solitary confinement, probably much like my grandfather when he was placed in his Hole to die. In Kansas, some of the state prisoners staged hunger strikes to try to shut down solitary confinement.

"They don't like solitude," the *Kansas City Star* said in a story rich in hyperbole. "The thoughts and shadows that dwell with lonely men drive them to fury and desperation. They would rather die than be forced to live apart from other men, each alone with himself. . . . They have taken all the solitude they can bear. . . . They made up their minds to die, if need be, to free themselves from solitary."

When Joseph Lyons arrived at the Kansas State Penitentiary, his prison mug shots showed a lean man, his hair greased back, a bit of a tough, unfazed in his striped khaki prison shirt. From behind bars, KSP Inmate No. 4022 occasionally wrote my grandfather and a favorite sister on Christmas Eve, and often to his mother. He also exchanged letters with Father McKenna back home at St. Thomas, unvanquished despite the flood, still promising salvation.

The family sometimes sent him small bits of cash, for cigarettes perhaps, and essentials like toothpaste. Money was tight during those Depression years, yet my grandfather once managed to send his older brother a one-dollar money order.

In a prison form filled out by the staff they noted that he was Irish and Catholic and that he had left school after the seventh grade. He told them he was a common laborer. He was just twenty-six years old.

Do you drink? Yes.

Smoke? Yes.

Chew? No.

Why did you leave home?

"Never left," he said.

Why not?

Life with mom, he said, is "pleasant."

They asked him about his crime.

"I broke into a house and took some things that did not belong to me."

They asked him one thing more: "What do you consider the main cause of your downfall?"

"Whiskey," he said.

He was paroled just before Christmas 1935, after serving almost two years of the five-year stretch. They placed him under the supervision of one of his sisters. The next year, 1936, Governor Alf M. Landon, at that time running as the hapless Republican presidential candidate against the immensely popular incumbent, Franklin Delano Roosevelt, granted Joseph a pardon. The governor and his state Board of Administration hoped he would do well. "It has been a pleasure to extend to you our friendly interest in your behalf," the prison records clerk, C. W. Wilson, wrote Joseph. "And now we wish for you a happy and successful future." Their well wishes were short-lived.

By then my grandfather was working as a janitor at the Menorah Hospital across the river in Kansas City, Missouri, and he helped Joseph land a job there, too. My grandfather swung a mop, and his brother washed windows. In an upstairs hospital suite at that time, the city boss, Tom Pendergast, was recovering from a colostomy. But the old man was not idle. From his hospital bed he accepted $10,000 in payoffs, and it became part of the evidence that would send him to prison.

Joseph was headed back to jail, too. Just before Thanksgiving he was arrested for stealing $142 in hospital supplies. It was the case I had uncovered in the storage caves in the bluffs on the Missouri River.

According to Joseph's account, he was angry over being fired for eating ice cream from the hospital cafeteria while off duty. Out of revenge he returned to the hospital kitchen before dawn and gathered up nearly anything in sight. He wrapped fifteen pieces of silverware and six napkins in a large tablecloth. On his way out he grabbed an electric Delco fan. He hid a Remington Rand office typewriter that he planned to steal later. He tossed most of the loot in the tablecloth and crept through the back door, stashing the goods deep among the tall grass under the nearby Troost Avenue bridge that spanned the city's Brush Creek. When he was caught he told police, "I got cold feet," and said he never went back to retrieve the spoils.

Sure enough, two witnesses turned him in. Austin Lawrence, a hospital supervisor, told police he thought he saw Joseph in there that morning. So did another witness, a Mrs. Waltmer, the hospital housekeeper who had fired him. Taken into custody, Joseph in November 1936 signed a one-page affidavit admitting his crime. His signature was more a scrawl. He began by saying he was thirty years old and single and that "I live with my mother Mary Lyons" in Kansas City, Kansas.

He was not, however, always candid. He shaved the truth a bit:

> I have never been in any trouble to speak of, with the exception of being arrested several times for being drunk. Until . . . I was given a sentence of one to five years at Lansing . . . and was paroled. Since that time I have not been in trouble of any kind, and worked at odd jobs around town when I was able to get them. In March of 1936 I went to work at Menorah Hospital as an assistant janitor, and worked at this place for about six months. I was discharged from this place for violating some of the rules of the hospital. Since that time I have not done much of anything with the exception of a few jobs that I was able to pick up.

On September 21, "I think it was about 4 a.m.," he said, "I went to the Menorah Hospital with the full intention of stealing something that I might be able to sell and get some money." He entered through the ambulance door, he said, and then wound his way to the dining room and started with the silverware and napkins. "I put it all in a tablecloth." Then it was to the nurse's office, "where I got an electric fan," before heading back outside. "These things I took out of the building and to a patch of weeds between the hospital and the bridge at about 50th and Troost. I hid those things in the weeds and went back to the hospital and took a typewriter from a nurse's desk at the end of the hall on the second floor. And as it was almost daylight I hid this machine in a patient's room on the first floor and covered it up with a mattress, intending to go back and get it later on." It was then that Joseph was tripped up. "As I was getting ready to leave the building, I was seen by Mrs. Waltmer. . . . She asked me what I was doing in the building and I told her I had come to borrow a street car pass. I left the building and went on home."

Now his Catholic conscience kicked in. "I got to thinking about being seen in the building by Mrs. Waltmer and got cold feet," he told police. "I did not go back to the woods after the articles I had hidden, fearing that I would get caught."

Weeks passed, and my uncle probably thought he was in the clear. He moved out of his rooming house near the hospital and returned across the river and settled back home with his mom. But then one night he showed up again at the rooming house to pick up some clothing he had left as collateral for his unpaid rent. The landlady tipped off the police. They arrested him on the porch. At Police Station No. 3 Joseph was told that if he signed the statement, it could be used against him. He scrawled his name on the bottom of the page anyway. "It is the truth," he said.

Again he pleaded guilty and because of the peculiarity of the crime, on the day he stood before the judge on a charge of grand larceny, the *Kansas City Star* carried the story at the top of its front page. The headline teased: "Revenge Leads to Jail." The press liked the little twist about Joseph being angry that he was fired for "eating ice cream off duty" and that he came back to get even. The paper added this postscript: "The hospital recovered the silverware and fan."

Joseph P. Lyons Jr. was sentenced to three years in prison, and this time they packed him off to the Missouri State Penitentiary in Jefferson City.

Missouri state prison records listed him as short with grayish green eyes and dark hair. By now he had this sallow complexion, the first signs of bone-white prison pallor. He also by then had come down with "syphilis, non-communicative." The guards measured his height and his weight; they even took his foot size—ten and a half inches.

He served a year and a half and was paroled in July 1938, under a "three-fourths law" that set him free on good behavior. The discharge forms were signed by Governor Lloyd C. Stark, who two years later ran for the Senate from Missouri but lost to future president Harry Truman. The governor, in granting Joseph's release, admonished him in the future "not to use intoxicating liquors."

A year later he was breaking into another home of a Lyons family neighbor in Kansas City, Kansas. This one belonged to Helen Pongretz, and he relieved her of her black pocketbook containing 60 cents, a bedspread, a scarf, two pillow cases, and, yes, another tablecloth. The total take was a pittance for all the risk he took, a mere $27.60. For a crook, Joseph Lyons sure had come down in stature.

Once again he was arrested, and once again he pleaded guilty. It was burglary and larceny from a dwelling all over again. It was back to the Kansas State Penitentiary, this time on a sentence of up to seven years.

Now in his mug shots he is thinner. He is gaunt. He is back in the prison striped shirt but now with his sunken cheeks, his hollow eyes, and an expression vacant and empty. Joseph P. Lyons Jr., the bumbler, the career petty thief, the kid asking to be caught, the older brother who could do no right.

Again the question: "What do you consider the main cause of your downfall?"

Again his answer: "Money and whiskey."

Again he was writing letters from prison, more than a hundred to his mother, dozens to some of his sisters, just one to the parish priest. He never wrote my grandfather. This is 1939 now and soon 1940, and my grandfather was lost, too, headed for Kansas City's skid row. On Joseph's prison records the warden's office noted that he did have a brother named James Lyons but as to where this brother lived, officials simply did not know. Authorities could find no fixed residence for James Lyons. So they simply made this notation for his address: "Add ??"

Joseph was assigned to C Cell House and the prison brickyard. Later his work record was upgraded, and his behavior was ranked "good." The warden's office moved him up to A Cell House, better quarters and other accommodations, supposedly. Next they transferred him to something called the "Old Crippled Men's Detail." Then he was sent to a prison hospital dormitory, and then to quarantine. There they diagnosed him with pulmonary tuberculosis.

On May 15, 1942, Warden M. F. Amrine wrote to my great-grandmother. The news was not good. "This morning," he said, "your son is gradually losing ground and there is little chance for his recovery."

Three days later, at half past seven in the evening, shrunken to 110 pounds, he died.

Mrs. Mary Lyons, who already had buried two daughters and just two months earlier her husband, returned to Mt. Calvary Cemetery. This time she could not afford another headstone, and so her first son, Joseph P. Lyons Jr., remains to this day somewhere in the family burial spot, minus a marker.

Without a marker his friends and family, my grandfather included, knew not where to gather on feast days to belt out the old Irish ballads, the "Danny Boy" of funerals that made them sway with drink, heel and heel and toe to toe, tilting their cans in loud, lusty, raucous song. "Oh, come what may / On St. Patrick's Day."

But there was no headstone to smash their empties, no marker to kick off the dirt. All that remained was the thin wisp of young Joseph's memory, the skinny, sallow kid dying alone in the prison infirmary. Joseph Lyons robbed houses and a hospital, too; he hid his loot in the tall, wet grass. And he always got caught. And like his younger brother, my grandfather, he ended his days in a life of little consequence.

Their mother went on to live another twelve years, long enough to suffer one more tragedy, the devastating Kansas City flood in the summer of 1951. This time it rained and it rained, nineteen inches of falling water recorded in one day alone. It rained so much the flood of 1903 was remembered as but a puddle; it made the water-logged basement at St. Thomas in 1903 a mere trickle. For weeks it rained, and then the swollen, angry Kansas River came barreling down upon Kansas City. The stockyards and packinghouses were drenched and flooded out. Fires burned for days. Homes and businesses went up in flames. Thousands lost their jobs; thousands more lost their homes. Mary lost hers.

St. Thomas Catholic Church was once more destroyed. More than twenty-five feet of water stood in the sanctuary. Some of the water rose so high it reached the choir loft. All would have been lost if not for this hearty group of Kansas parishioners. They joined forces scooping out the sanctuary and pumping out the basement. On Sundays they carried folding chairs down to the basement and once again knelt on the still-damp floor; there they broke the Holy Bread. And all above them once more the workers were cleaning up the old brown-brick church, drying it out. But now they laid rubber tile flooring, lest it rain a third time. Women scrubbed, and the members of the church Altar Society repainted. When they were done they did what all good Catholics do. They held an ice cream social.

Mary Lyons moved in with a daughter, and finally, in 1954, just short of her eightieth birthday, when I was but a year old, she died of heart failure. Then what was left of the Lyons clan trooped back to the cemetery, and there they buried the matriarch alongside the rest of her loved ones. In death, at last, they were all together—all but one, her second son. He sleeps down the hill.

CHAPTER 4

In the spring of 1948 when my grandfather was killed in his prison, the Lyons family plot was full, so they buried him down a long slope in Mt. Calvary's old section. Alone much of his life, he lies alone in eternity.

Some years later as a young boy, my cousin Rick Neumann would join his family for visits to the cemetery on Decoration Day. "We'd leave flowers, and I'd ask my dad, 'Who was James Lyons? Why is he over here all by himself?' My dad always said he couldn't remember or he didn't really know. Or he didn't want to tell. They were a very old-fashioned family. Some things were not spoken."

Even in his newspaper obituary the family tried to hide the truth. Just as they had for his brother Joseph Jr., they said my grandfather had died at home. But maybe that is true, I thought. He lived the last of his life drifting on the streets of Kansas City, pretty much homeless. In the city jail he would have had a bed and sheets, and a warm meal. Even in solitary confinement, if nothing else he had four walls around him and the spare mattress. Home was where he laid his head, crouched up against the winter wind or lying sweating in the morning sun.

James Lyons followed his father into the rail yards and the packinghouses. He butchered meat, and he later moved to the Missouri side of Kansas City and pushed a broom at that Menorah Hospital. He hired himself out as a common laborer. Somewhere along the way he sold beer or peanuts at the baseball game. He went through girlfriends and wives about as frequently as hangovers. He and Helen had two children, Edythe Ruth and Joseph. When he left Helen, she put Edythe up for adoption, but Helen continued to care for the boy, long suffering from seizures and cerebral palsy. He never saw them again.

Edythe Ruth was renamed Barbara, and in the mid-1990s she contacted our family for the first time. She showed me a copy of her original birth certificate. It noted that even at her birth James Lyons was already separated from his first wife. He was identified as "James Pat Lyons." He was living back at home with his parents in Kansas City, Kansas. But he was working, the document said; in fact, it stated he had worked for six years as a meat cutter in one of the city's packinghouses. She called us because like my mother, who was deceased by then, she wanted to know something of their father. Who was he?

It turned out that what she had been told about James Lyons and passed on to me was far wide of the mark. "He was an alcoholic, I guess, and died in a jail falling out of his bunk," she said she had been told. "Hit his head, I heard."

I tried to contact Barbara recently, to tell her the truth as I now know it, to tell her there was no prison bunk and no falling to the floor. But I was too late in reaching her; Barbara had died in 2002.

After leaving Barbara's mother, James Lyons met my grandmother. Their marriage in November 1930 produced two children. Mary Elizabeth Lyons, my mother, was born in September 1931. They lived on East Seventh Street in the city's Northeast section, the apartment building long gone now. My mother had told me she was born at home. In fact, she said, she was born on the kitchen table. I thought that was odd. But on a trip to the Missouri state capital in Jefferson City I obtained a copy of her birth certificate, and sure enough she was right—about being born at home anyway. The document also noted that James R. Lyons (they had his middle initial wrong) had worked the last three months as a janitor at the National Bellas Hess building. He must have gotten that job through his mother-in-law, Rose Toelle Norman. She worked there for years as a telephone switchboard operator. The warehouse was built in 1913 in North Kansas City, situated just over the Missouri River amid that area's grain elevators and railroad switching yards. It was a catalog and retail operation, nine stories of hardwood floors on Armour Road where merchandise was stored before it was shipped out to customers.

My grandparents' second and last child was born in July 1933. They named him James Norman Lyons. By then they were living in an apartment at Fifth and Myrtle streets, a two-story clapboard building with a wraparound porch. On the boy's birth certificate my grandfather was identified as "an out of work laborer." The job sweeping up at the catalog plant was gone, I guess. So was the meat-packing job. And soon enough he was gone, too, his second marriage over. He vanished, and he never returned.

My grandmother sued him for divorce, claiming "indignities and desertion," and the marriage was dissolved in December 1934. She was awarded the "care, custody and control" of the two children, and he was ordered to pay "the costs," whatever that might amount to in the teeth of the Great Depression.

I found copies of the divorce papers in the river caves along with other old Jackson County records. One evening I read the five-paragraph divorce decree several times over, just to make sure I had not missed something. I read it again, and then read it probably ten times more until finally it felt like a dagger had sunk in. I had skipped over one short legal phrase that turned out to be the most telling of all. It said that while my grandmother had appeared in court in person and with a lawyer, "the defendant comes not." He did not even bother to show up.

So Zillah, like her mother, was left to raise two children—a daughter and a son. She moved back in with her mother, and soon she too took her seat on the bus, joining her at the National Bellas Hess catalog center, a long, dreary ride up Prospect Avenue and over the river and into the grimy grain and rail district of North Kansas City. Then at nightfall another bus home, to two more husbands, and an unhappy life, the shadowy life, in a house near mine that I was not allowed to visit. Because James Lyons, the man she loved first, the man in the November 1930 wedding photograph, had run off. He was the man she was clutching tightly as she smiled brightly in the photo, heady stuff for a woman who rarely smiled in any of the other photographs. And she would speak precious little of him again.

I hunted in the caves for any more court documents into whether he made good on child support or alimony payments, or whether she had to sue him for funds or even take him to the county prosecutor on criminal charges of wife and child abandonment. I did find a March 1939 court notice that a suit brought by Zillah and her mother, Rose, against James Lyons was dismissed "for want of prosecution." That would mean either he paid them some money or they gave up trying to hold him responsible. Part of the problem was that he had moved across the state line and back to his parents' home in Kansas City, Kansas, making it all the more difficult for my grandmother to force him to appear in a court in Missouri. He would have known that was a good and safe place to hide.

While in the caves I did make copies of other wife and child abandonment cases brought by Jackson County prosecutors against deadbeat dads. It helped me understand the despair of mothers set adrift during the harsh years of the Depression. The records were stuffed in large cardboard boxes of prosecutors' case files from the 1930s and 1940s, one box for each month, and probably fifty files in each box. The papers were brittle and filled with dirt and limestone dust, and probably a third of the files in each box were wife and child abandonment cases. Those numbers alone showed me how desperate the times had been.

Raymond and Virginia Greene had three daughters—Dawine, Virginia Lee, and Mary Delores. Their ages ranged from seven to four years old, and when their father left the house, the family went on the government dole. "I am employed as a housemaid at 3435 Olive for Mrs. Ketchum and she pays me $12 a week," the girls' mother told the judge in a handwritten affidavit. "I have no other employment. My husband left me in March. He went to Gary, Indiana, as far as I know. His mother lives at Cherokee, Kansas. She says she doesn't know where he is at. I have not seen my husband since the funeral of his sister at Cherokee [two years ago]. He was an able-bodied man the last I saw him."

On went the files, a broken family on each page. Eslie Sims had been in and out of jails for drinking and vagrancy, for marijuana use, for stealing and burglary. He took off for Michigan. Jack McKay wiped out the family's Commerce Trust Company account, leaving just $41. "That is all the money I have to support my children," said his wife, Viola, a mother of two. She was making $1.75 an hour.

For my grandfather, there was never a hint that he ever paid a dime to support his family or bothered to visit. His son carried his own name, James Lyons, and his daughter, Mary, was named after his mother, and still he never returned home.

He married a third time to a woman named Mary and after her a fourth bride, this a Josephine. She was the one listed on his death certificate and also identified in the city directory as his last wife. But his family did not include her in his newspaper obituary.

They also did not list the four children he had from his first two marriages. And apparently little if anything came from the last two wives; I could find no trace of any children born to them. The man was gone.

Over the years he stayed on both sides of the Missouri River in the expanding metropolitan area, in Missouri and in Kansas. He rented apartments and boarded with families. He briefly lived with his older brother, Joseph Jr. For a while he moved in with his parents. Along the way he lost ambition and hope, probably any lust for life. Except for the raised glass. He was, like my grandmother said, lovable in his cups—a drinker, not a fighter; a bum and not a husband. The booze had him, and the booze did not let go.

James Lyons wound up at Fifth and Main streets, what was once the storied heart of the old city and now its neglected skid row. There he joined a crumpled army of broken men, women too, sometimes children as well, the nameless, the aimless, for some the blameless, those who the Irish say never "go on the dry."

Inside the pubs the whiskey flowed freely, and all were welcomed with heart and hand. There they raised a famous Irish toast, shouting from the bar tops, "Let us fill our cans!"

No doubt he joined in their merriment, to laugh and to drink and to forget the human debris, the wives and the children and the jobs he had left scattered in his wake. My grandfather bent his elbow. He filled his can.

The Depression was claiming whole families, sending husbands and sons adrift. By 1933, around the time James Lyons left my grandmother, at least twenty-five thousand families in the United States had split up, and some two million young men and boys were afoot. In Kansas City, nine thousand families were on relief. That number doubled in 1935. Three years later one of every eight men who were strong enough to work needed public assistance. When things hit bottom, fifteen hundred tramps a day passed through Kansas City.

Yet as Depression-era cities went, Kansas City fared better than others. Work could still be found in the rail yards because the cattle still had to be shipped to market, and the packinghouses were brimming because people still had to eat. With graft and underhanded city contracts, Boss Tom Pendergast kept his cement company churning and many out of the breadlines and gainfully employed. No applecarts for them; he found them work on new roads and bridges around town. For still others, the out-of-work and the homeless and those down and out, he served up Christmas dinners.

Kansas City outlasted the Depression because the place was notoriously wide open. These were the 1930s, the last pangs of Prohibition, and the dry laws were still in force. But Prohibition had no seat at the bar in Kansas City. An empty can was not welcome here.

So the town, indignant as always, became a magnet for drifters, for bawdy piano players and jazz musicians who jammed all night, and strippers who doffed and wiggled and bowed above the smoke-ringed tables. Out on the nightclub floor topless cocktail waitresses served drinks wearing see-through cellophane bottoms, their pubic hair shaved in the shape of playing cards—hearts and diamonds for some of the ladies, clubs and spades for others.

Jazz and cocktails and chorus girls entertained well into the evening. Gambling dens and bookie joints seldom closed. The roulette wheel was always a-spin. If you wanted to see sin, the saying went, forget Paris or Chicago or New York. Come to Kansas City.

The red-light district ran for blocks; in some places girls could be had for a quarter. Fifty cents tops. You chose your girl from a storefront window, like Macy's at Christmas. By 1930 some 250 houses of prostitution, their lights turned low, were filled to the upstairs bedrooms, and no police officers or vice squad seemed able or willing to shut them down. Speakeasies popped up on nearly every downtown street corner. The city was hot during the day and on fire at night. The party never shut down. "A happy town," recalled Count Basie in an understatement as light as his touch on the keyboard.

Out on the rural post roads of Jackson County the party partied through the night at last-call spots known as "gallon houses." They sprung up for anyone wanting one more tug for the road. Places in Lone Jack and Oak Grove packed them in. Whiskey was hauled in by the barrelful. The booze was poured into large glass bottles or sold in earthen jugs. Stop for a drink, and stay a while. Stay for a long while.

Occasionally, federal revenue agents tried to break up the party. Once they dumped five barrels of Jamaican ginger extract used to cook hooch into the Missouri River at the foot of Main Street. The barrels were seized at a railroad warehouse after the wholesale drug company that had consigned for the shipment failed to pick it up.

But five barrels, about 250 gallons in all, was no big loss. The newspaper had only one lament. "The poor fish," the paper said.

On rare occasions, more for show than anything else, the G-men rounded up bootleggers and crowded them into a holding cell in the downtown federal building. They let the press photographers in to have at them. They had great names, these men, names like Tudie Pasano and Noxie La Barber. They sported bowler hats and natty suits and bright polka-dot ties. The guards did not bother to take their fingerprints or dress them in prison jumpsuits because lawyers were already rushing down to bail them out. One of the men waited idly in the cell, drumming his fingers. Another chomped on a cigar.

My grandfather was in and out of jails, too. He did not supply the stuff; he did not mix it or brew it or sell it to others. He drank it. A drunk, he was. He would have been one of the bootleggers' more dependable customers, though he probably could afford nothing more than the cheapest bottle. Like many young, impressionable men he kept falling easily under the spell of alcohol. The charm swept him up, swallowed him up, and carried him off. He could not resist its pull. Over and over again the whiskey rolled and the cans were filled and the hangovers greeted the morning. People around town called them the "whiskey crowd."

Off with them he marched, learning to drink with the best, I suppose, to spike more than his morning coffee. By noon he was spiking his Golden Mist soda—if he was up by noon, if he was awake at all, if he could even afford the soda. And why would he want to dilute his whiskey anymore? Skip the coffee; skip the Golden Mist, too. His nights were his, and they ended only when the sun rose. His days began when one of his thin, glazed eyes cracked painfully open.

Nationally, the city was both praised and scorned. The *New Republic* magazine noted that Kansas City was the nation's second-largest packing center and also dubiously claimed the highest divorce rate outside of Reno, Nevada. The city was lined with miles of railroad tracks and a thousand freight cars parked end to end. It sported the finest horse show outside of Dublin and one of the most crooked Irish Catholic Democratic political leaders around. And still, the magazine said, they persevered. "Their hearts are as big as their prairies."

And the whiskey flowed.

And we filled our cans.

"Drinking is universal and joyous," said the *New Republic*. "Only the wealthy have real or imitation scotch; but oceans of very good 'cornlicker' . . . slip down the Kansas City gullet. High school boys tote hip-flasks."

On the other end of the state, prudish St. Louis looked down on its sister city. "Rackets of all kinds flourish," decried the *St. Louis Post-Dispatch*. "Saloons boastingly proclaim, 'we never close.'" The paper warned that "the poor are quite as privileged to lose their money as the rich. The democracy of corruption knows no caste. The unbolted doors swing a welcome to everybody."

Even when the Prohibition laws were repealed in 1933 the *Kansas City Star* reported that the city greeted the change with one giant civic shrug. Who cared? Prohibition had never slowed the booze. Prohibition was for the rest of the country. No liquor laws applied here. Local political figures hoisted their own pints and led the way. They were known as "booze-o-crats," and they filled their cans, too.

"John Barleycorn's ghost, the bootleg liquor, danced a slow sad piece in Kansas City bars last night," the *Star* reported when Prohibition ended and liquor was "legal" again. "Everybody yawned. "

Others who enjoyed a neighborly snort during those Prohibition years became so fond of the roadside booze that they pledged never to return to the good stuff. Not a drop of port for them, not a sip of sherry. A little "red straight" would do just fine. Fourteen years of Prohibition went down the drain, and no one in Kansas City seemed to notice or care.

By 1940, when the Second World War replaced the Depression and for many the party lights started to twinkle and go out, my grandfather would by then have been staggering shoulder-bent among the other town drunks. Once he had found courage in a cup; now whiskey had wrecked his life. He could not or would not stop drinking. Prosperity returned to Kansas City, and it passed him by. War came with Pearl Harbor, and the army looked elsewhere. Soldiers came home to jobs and new families and new opportunities, and no one hired the town drunk, James Patrick Lyons. His good times had passed him by.

Fifteen years it was since he had left our family, and he marked them largely on the street and in the barrooms and alone somewhere with his precious bottle. He went on one very long drunk. By the spring of 1948 and his last arrest for intoxication, he had already been picked up some eighty times by the police—always for vagrancy and public drunkenness.

The police found him in bushes, they found him on sidewalks, and they found him zigzagging down the street, ricocheting feet plowing into light poles and fire hydrants, tripping over the curb. They found him facedown in the storm grates and next to garbage cans. They found him huddled against the back doors of liquor stores. They found him under lamplights in the evening and under the harsh glare of tomorrow's noonday sun. They found him belly-up at the bar one minute, and belly-down the next.

He was what the Christian relief workers at the City Union Mission at Fifth and Main streets saw each morning on the sidewalks and side alleys, in the bushes and on the benches, too, where he and the others had collapsed from utter exhaustion after another night of drinking and carousing amid a shamble of abandoned buildings, faded nightspots and failing neon. He was to them "one of God's human sparrows." But when the police came or the relief workers stooped to offer a helping hand, all of them, my grandfather included, scattered like crows.

The neighborhood of Fifth and Main, his last home on the streets, had been the birthplace of Kansas City, once the town's civic center and its commercial district. In the late 1800s a prominent life insurance company started writing policies and employing scores of people on Main Street. Storefronts flung open their doors to crowds of customers. The town was alive with color. Wild Bill Hickok, Bat Masterson, and Buffalo Bill—all rode through this Kansas City footprint at Fifth and Main.

Fortunes were quickly made and quickly lost in the city still being born, and the criminal element knew exactly how to get its slice of the action. And right from the start the police left a lot of crimes unsolved. The *Star,* in its very first edition on September 18, 1880, reported about a "daring highway robbery." "Last night about 10 o'clock," went the paper's story on page 4 of its premier edition, "a man whose name could not be learned was knocked down and dragged into the alley running from Fourth to Fifth street, west of Main. The cries of the assaulted man awoke the cook of the Barnum Hotel, whose sleeping room is immediately over the locality where the assault occurred. The cook cried lustily for the police; the assailants hurriedly scampered off."

Frank's Hall anchored Fifth and Main; it became the city's first major theater. It had this giant panoramic painting of Ireland, a wonder for all to see. Fiery Irish nationalists came and spoke onstage. But what really drew the crowds were Tom Thumb and the equally pint-sized Commodore McNutt who stepped out from behind the curtain at Frank's. Even back then the bizarre checkmated politics.

Out on the street Thomas Phelan, a big Irish patriot and a marksman with a rifle, dazzled the people with his ability to shoot the bowl off a pipe in a man's mouth. For a time they called Fifth and Main "Battle Row," as horses and carriages and men armed with pistols fought over the right-of-way on the mud-chunked streets and plywood sidewalks. The churches lost out to the saloons. And the saloons competed with the brothels. "Upstairs apartments" for gentlemen were furnished with mirrors, private bars, and fashionable Brussels carpets. The carpets were soft and thick, and they did not leave rug burns.

Annie Chambers was the grandest madam of all—until she found religion. She ran her bordello until 1923, a wayfarer's spot for gold prospectors en route to the Rockies and cattlemen herding beef up from Texas. By the time she closed her door thousands of young ladies had entertained male guests in her establishment. "I bought them fine clothes, showed them how to do their hair and taught them manners," she said of her girls.

Miss Annie ended her life alone, nearly blind, sitting away the days in what once was her front parlor with the circular settee and the chairs done up in leather. "Several of my girls of the old days come to see me still," she told a reporter in her last interview, in 1934. "I have them read the Bible to me." She died in the house a year later, alone in her big brass bed.

Bob Potee ran two gambling parlors, and often he personally dealt the cards. He remains a mythical figure to this day; a few old accounts of him have his last name spelled as Poteet. His game was high-stakes faro, and quite a man of spirit was Bob. He strutted up and down Fifth and Main in immaculate attire, an ensemble that included a gold-headed cane and high silk stovepipe hat. He had this great Prince Albert coat. In my grandfather's time another town character would emerge to walk these same streets in his own grand style. But for now it was good old Mr. Bob Potee. He always wore black, and they called him the Prince of the Dealers.

He insisted on honesty inside his gambling clubs just off Main Street. He promised fair hands and square deals. "Cheating is a practice far removed from my name," he liked to proclaim. "Neither gentlemen nor hog thieves speak of it in my presence."

But nothing lasts, and eventually the city center started climbing farther south up the hard river bluffs, moving away from Fifth and Main, and the shop owners and the businessmen and the customers and tourists too began to abandon the old historic area. The fabled street corner started to crumple from lost revenue. Shops closed, stores shuttered their doors, and For Sale signs went up in the windows. The city was leaving behind its first home for larger prospects up the hill. Potee saw his parlors go under. Soon his faro table stood empty.

So one day he scribbled a short note. "Plant me decent," he wrote. He fitted himself out in hat and cane and Prince Albert jacket. All dressed in black was Bob as he strolled north on Main, his back to the growing city and the new buildings and progress taking shape up on the bluffs behind him. Five blocks and he reached the water's edge, the thick, muddy Missouri that had brought them all to this city of rivers to begin with. There, they say, he kept on walking.

Sic transit gloria Bob Potee.

Only the skeletons remained from the Old Town. Two other whorehouses also once the pride of their time, Madame Lovejoy's and the Eva Prince resort, stood empty for years save for the termites and the drunks. Dust covered the once stately ballrooms, and the winter wind crackled through the chipped, painted glass. Upstairs the bedrooms were closed and locked. The old metal bedsprings turned to rust, heard no more to click and clack like the passenger trains at night.

By 1940 the neighborhood was blighted with vacant buildings and teetering walls. Shops had been torn down, and the back alleys harbored the ghosts of the old days. Eight years later, when my grandfather had taken up residence in its street lots strewn with broken bottles or when he had the pocket change for a room, the wind carried the whisper of that lost grandeur.

Up and down Fifth and Main, lurching his way toward another bottle or a warm Dumpster to crawl under, this is what he saw through his bloodshot, bleary eyes:

At 534 Main—St. Christopher's Inn. The Christian mission helped feed the drunks and homeless, and they served up annual Thanksgiving and Christmas dinners, hot turkey plates and steamed rolls. On Christmas 1946, my grandfather's next to last, they fed fifteen hundred people.

St. Christopher's was a refuge for indigent men sponsored by the Catholic diocese. "Harbor the Harborless," ran its motto. It was managed by an Irishman named John O'Brien, a salty fellow with a thick Celtic accent, ten years older than my grandfather. Over a span of twenty years he helped feed and clothe tens of thousands of men. By 1960 he had provided Christian burials for 170. He did not discriminate. "If a guy needs a pair of pants," O'Brien would say, "he needs them no matter his religion."

At 536 Main—Our Lady of the Highway Chapel. This was a Catholic church next to St. Christopher's. Here my grandfather could pray, if he prayed at all. (We humans do pray the needier we are.) It had been an old warehouse building renovated into a church. The entire first floor was reproduced to look like a chapel near Bois, France. For centuries the French church was a wayside stop for travelers. The chapel on Main had a knotty-pine interior, and the wall work and friezes were made to resemble the medieval chapels of Europe. It was all quite fancy for the common man. But usually more men huddled outside rather than wander in. On the church steps God might send you a handout.

There was Mom's Lunch at 532 Main and the Minute Coffee House next door. A package store was open at 552 Main, called the Riverside Buffet Liquor, and a bar called Bird's Place. Most prominent on the block was the City Union Mission at 537 Main Street.

By the late 1940s skid row hit bottom, if a bottom there was, and volunteers at the mission valiantly still tried saving souls. It was a harrowing task, and relief worker Maurice Vanderberg recalled his path each morning from downtown north to the mission chapel at Fifth and Main. His thoughts were recorded by Juliana Vanderberg-Rohlfing in her history of the mission, *I Never Asked for the Easy Way.* "I crossed Ninth Street in the shadow of the Kay Hotel," he said, "counting down the street numbers to the Nelson Building, which housed City Union Mission."

It was there I discovered the bodies. Some were propped in doorways. Some sprawled full-length across the sidewalk. Some lay with legs stretched into the street. They weren't dead, for there was movement and even strange unintelligible sounds from a few.

From the gaping doorways of near-collapsing caverns came an alien din and a suffocating odor. Strange, unreal figures staggered in and out to add to the noise or to join their fellows on the sidewalk. And I was scared.

   . . . Seventh Street . . .

Sixth Street . . .

One more block and I would be there. What would I find? What kind of people were these who would spend their lives in this hell? And for what?

They were the pair of young boys who knocked on the mission door one blustery winter's night, one of the lads dressed in little more than a thin cotton shirt.

"Why would your mother allow you to come out in such cold weather?" a relief worker asked.

The boy was too embarrassed to answer, so his friend spoke up.

"Aw," the friend said, "she's drunk all the time."

They were Scotty the "Notorious Scotchman." He was, the mission said, "a man of unusual intelligence and an uncontrollable thirst for booze." For a time he curled up in one of the closed brothels, climbing through the old trap door and down to the abandoned wine cellar below. It was like a solitary cell. But Scotty did not mind. It smelled perfect, he said.

They were Edna, who showed up at the mission asking for a cot for the night. They helped her to the bedroom, watching in pain as she labored up the stairs. When they put her to bed they noticed the deep black bruises across her back. Edna said she supposed some policeman had beaten her while she was drunk. Or so she thought. They gave her warm clothes and blankets, but it could not defeat a severe cold. In a few days she was dead.

By the time of my grandfather's last winter, January 1948, old skid row was derided as "gandy row." The mission was serving 120,000 meals to the drunks and homeless. They provided 9,000 beds and 175 pairs of shoes. But only a little over a thousand of the down-and-out asked for prayers, and of them only 235 were converted.

Often, instead, the police moved in. "No floaters," the cops called out, cracking heads. "Get to work or get out of the city." In one raid they booked 94 men on charges of vagrancy or intoxication, filling up the black patrol wagons for trips to headquarters. Kansas City police chief Henry W. Johnson vowed to return the next day. "We're putting a stop to this, now and for keeps," the chief promised.

At Municipal Court the dockets filled to bursting. Out at the Municipal Farm the guards took in record numbers of new inmates. But many of the drunks simply shuffled east to Troost Avenue and The Paseo. One sidewalk is as comfortable to sleep on as any other, they said.

Nevertheless the *Star* hailed the "cleanup" patrols. They wanted more raids. "It is the old, old problem of floating men who have to go somewhere and cause trouble wherever they go," the newspaper editorialized. "The police broom is the device that gets the job done."

Eventually, the drunks moved back. Post–World War II inflation was up, and the cost of living was hitting those on the street all the harder. A three-egg breakfast was no longer a dime, and a T-bone steak, the hottest draw on the menu at Bob's Lunch at 607 Main, was up to seventy cents.

But those who ran the lunch counters and the skid row diners knew it was the booze and not the blue-plate specials that drew their customers. So they kept certain prices down. Wine still sold for thirty-five cents a pint, and it was known as "the fastest selling liquor in the cement gully" of Fifth and Main.

To keep their taverns and package stores busy, the barkeeps hung "No Women Allowed" signs in their windows. Females, they said, only hurt business. "Seventy-five percent of the fellows who are down and out and drinking can trace their trouble to a woman," one bartender complained. "We don't intend to remind them by having women hanging around." Keep the women out and the cans filled, and "our trade doesn't cause anybody any trouble."

One drunk readily agreed. "If the housing situation wasn't so bad, I'd get married. Look at the money you'd save," he said. His clothing hung on him, and he smelled of the street. He wore a ragged suit, shoes with holes in the toes, and a shirt collar held down by safety pins. He was not being dressed by a woman, that was clear, and he was not going to be dressed down by one, either.

Skid row, gandy row, no women allowed—call it what you will, the area persevered. My grandfather in his last days was staying at the Fox Hotel at 548 Main, in a room above a bar called Bird's Place. The Fox had served as a bunkhouse for years, with its five-story front facade taken from the style of New Orleans' French Quarter. It also was famous for ghosts.

Back in 1917, eighty-six people who said they lived there voted in the city elections, though in that year the hotel was vacant and boarded up. Phantom voters were they. In 1946 the hotel was re-opened, a very seedy place, and twenty-one men were registered to vote as residents in the August primary. In truth not a single one of them actually lived there. The Fox was nothing more than a flophouse for transients, and it was torn down a few years later along with other buildings in the old district to make room for a Sixth Street expressway.

But before the Fox was gone, it was my grandfather's last home—not counting the Municipal Farm. And one of his last roommates on the row was Kirby McRill, a bearded, long-haired Irishman who regularly strode up and down skid row, wherever his blistered feet would carry him. He became the heir to the man who walked before him, the bankrupt card dealer and faro master, poor old Bob Potee.

McRill called himself the "Unkissed Farmer and Walking Marvel." Whereas Potee twirled a cane, McRill pushed a handcart. He passed the boarded-up windows and the faded neon, the chipped sidewalks and dark alleys and the vacant lots, filling his basket with scrap metal, tin cans, and paper cartons. Collecting trash for resale was his livelihood.

He came from a farm near Reno, Kansas. He was a confirmed bachelor and did not care much for farming, either. What he liked to do was walk. He walked the three miles into town. He walked to Lawrence, home of the state university. He walked to Tonganoxie and Leavenworth and finally he walked to Kansas City.

He wore heavy shoes to keep down the blisters. To keep out the sun he plopped atop his head a misshapen cowboy hat. To keep the gnats off his legs he wore long wool stockings and knickerbockers, too. He had all kinds of reasons for walking. To Reno to buy supplies, he said, where he would purchase a loaf of bread and ice cream for lunch and scoop it down, and then head back for home. He would walk to Leavenworth to pay his taxes. He went to Kansas City to start a new life.

Once a car came along and slowed, and the driver peered out the window at the odd-looking walking man. He offered Kirby a ride.

"No, thanks," McRill said. "I'm in a hurry."

By the time he hit Kansas City at some point in the 1920s he was already fifty years old. His feet were not just tired; they were ancient. Still he kept walking. He participated in Heart of America walkathons around Kansas City. In an era when other communities on the East and West coasts had flagpole sitters, Kansas City had Kirby McRill.

Once he put a notice in the newspaper calling himself the Man Who Never Gets Tired. "I am a man of steel," he proclaimed. "I do not know what fatigue is.

Kirby walked and walked and walked some more. He talked about crossing the United States one step at a time, from the Pacific Coast. Getting across the desert would be pretty tricky, and that idea fell by the roadside. Another time they held a walk race downtown, with Kirby McRill facing off against the legendary George Brown, who hailed himself as "the World's Champion Walker." A crowd filled the sidewalks as the two contestants took off up Main and out to Eleventh, to Petticoat Lane and Grand Avenue. They circled around the Orpheum Theater. Halfway into it Kirby started to fall behind. Thinking no one was paying close attention, he broke into a dogtrot.

"Kirby, man, you're running! You're running!" yelled a bystander.

"I can't help it," he puffed back. "I can't let him get ahead of me."

He told everyone he had come to Kansas City to find a woman. Romance was what he was walking for. He found it first in Daisy Belle Hicks. She was a coed at a local barber college. For three years they wooed one another, and then suddenly out of nowhere she ran off with the barber. She dumped McRill hard. So hard that my grandfather and the other bums could hear him walking about the streets in a long face, crying, "Throw out the lifeline, someone's sinking today."

He went to court and sued her for $250,000. Breach of promise, he said. The lawsuit, of course, went nowhere, but Kirby sure did. He walked all the more, up and down city streets, but mostly the sidewalks of skid row. Here he pushed his metal cart, collecting scrap and letting his hair and whiskers grow out. Grow they did—long and scraggly and impossible to tame. The mess covered his head and face, the brown-red snarls and handlebar mustache like an aura, a halo maybe, for all to see following Kirby McRill. Jilted in love, he swore off all barbershops. He vowed never to shave or cut his hair until he was kissed again. So the years passed and his step slowed, and still he trudged on.

Then one day another pretty lady caught his eye, and Kirby announced he was "half in love." He told skid row that he planned to cut off half of his hair and half of his beard. But she left him too, and now sad-eyed and brokenhearted Kirby McRill swore off women of all kinds.

The man was well into his seventies by now. Drivers often honked when he wandered in front of cars. An automobile slightly bumped him on the street. Two years hence, at the age of seventy-five, he would be struck by a car, and he was killed. He died just like my grandfather; the accident broke his neck. A crowd rushed over and saw his pushcart upside down, the wheels still spinning. They buried him back near Reno, Kansas. He had all of $3.30 to his name and a stack of IOUs. Four hundred people attended his funeral. "Occasionally there lives a man who is different," said the preacher.

In his last days it was not the cars or the drivers that worried Kirby McRill. His nemesis, he said, were stray dogs with big teeth and the drunks who bothered him incessantly. Like the gnats, they were. For kicks the drunks would try to clip strands of his long hair and save them for souvenirs, maybe sell them even, usually to find themselves sprawled on the sidewalk for their trouble.

But the hair and the beard that Kirby prized above everything else would not last forever. Nothing does. Arrested by the police for repeated acts of vagrancy he was fined the outlandish sum of $250, and that meant a trip to the Kansas City Municipal Farm. There, out of spite, the guards cut his hair and shaved his beard. He protested vehemently, and it took five strong men to hold him down. But Kirby McRill's locks were shorn and his beard was shaved, and he returned to Fifth and Main with a pathetic patch of stubble. That jail, everyone agreed, was no place to be.

CHAPTER 5

If you died on the streets, they more than likely delivered your body to the potter's field next to the Kansas City Municipal Farm. They wrapped you up in newspapers, and inmates dug your grave. The pauper's cemetery was a sloping two-acre tract, and over the years more than a thousand metal markers were shoved into the yellow clay, each carrying a slip of paper bearing a name and a number because sometimes prisoners were buried there, too. Other corpses came from Fifth and Main, still others from the city morgue where officials kept them two, three . . . up to five years hoping someone might claim the bodies. "They'd bring out these boxes, flimsy as the dickens," once recalled an old-time prisoner after the ancient jail was torn down and the cemetery weeded over. "They were stained red, looked a little like cigar boxes, and we'd dig the holes and put them in." To save space, some boxes were buried on top of other boxes, and some prisoners would pop the lids open first, just to steal a peek inside. "I never liked to look," he said. "But I always did."

The warden was Cyriel Provyn—his official title was "superintendent." He came to the Farm in 1941. He lived alone in a modest little house on the prison grounds, divorced and childless, more a farmer than a warden. He wore horn-rimmed glasses, greased his hair back, and put on pounds around his midsection—a dead ringer for the warden in that prison movie *The Shawshank Redemption*. Provyn shut down potter's field in 1968. Soon after that the city announced the whole prison was coming down to make room for a more modern penal institution. The new place would house mostly the mentally ill; drunks from now on would be turned over to city and charitable agencies. The hope was to wean them off the bottle rather than punish them for what new evidence showed was a physical disease. If alcoholism could be treated, lives could be saved. Reform was in the air.

But Provyn was a man of the old world. He closed the cemetery, and the prison building was torn down and he retired. For a while he served on the Downtown Optimist Club, and one year he was elected club president. He often wondered about the misspent lives both out at the prison Farm and under the ground. "The people in the cemetery don't mean much to the world," the warden once reminisced. "No friends or family to speak of."

When he left the Farm for a suburban home in Leawood, Kansas, Provyn had some fleeting words for his prisoners, too. "My first love is those men out there, the work and the institution," he said, sixty-nine years old at his retirement, his life's work done, Provyn moving out and the prison coming down. But he acknowledged that many of his men never made good on life, and that they just kept returning to the Farm on alcohol charges time and time again. "In lots of cases it doesn't do any good. But we don't give up. We help the man who's been drunk 1,000 times as much as the man who has been drunk once. We try just as hard."

The inmate who helped bury many of the prisoners and paupers in the potter's graveyard, Arthur Jones by name, also reflected on the end of an era at the Municipal Farm. Jones was one of those fellows who kept being sentenced back to the jail, so many times that he and Provyn estimated that he had served some twenty years as Provyn's "houseboy" there. In his gray overalls he told reporters, "Lordy, it makes you think about living and dying."

The prison's main building was a ghost-white castlelike structure rising two hundred feet atop a hill southeast of downtown. Driving up winding Ozark Road, climbing the slow-rising crest, a visitor found the structure almost medieval, quite imposing in size, shining in its native limestone walls yet dark and foreboding within.

The idea was hatched years earlier. One of the first town jails in Kansas City was built in 1853, a two-room, fourteen-by-sixteen-foot structure. They called it a workhouse, and it primarily dealt with petty offenders, debtors, vagrants, and the like. But the building just housed them; it did not work them at all, and it taught them no new skills. When their sentences were up it turned them out as shiftless and as ornery as when they went in. The word *corrections* had not yet been invented.

In 1872, when Fifth and Main was in its heyday, a second city jail was opened, and within ten years it too was deemed "appalling." Male prisoners were housed in overcrowded wooden cells. Separate locks and keys held them in. Fire loomed as an everyday potential hazard. Vermin and rodents infested the place. There was little air and less proper diet. By 1896 Mayor James M. Jones pardoned a number of the prisoners; it was too unsafe and too inhumane to keep them there.

One of the lucky inmates heading home was Harry C. Howell; he had a lot of homes to go to. Howell had eight wives in eight states, they said. He had been sentenced to the workhouse for carrying concealed weapons, and Mayor Jones released him on the promise that he clear out in twenty-four hours.

"The place is simply horrible and no man can appreciate its horrors who has not seen it," a county grand jury concluded in a unanimously adopted report after investigating conditions there. "It is a disgrace to the city that it has been tolerated all these years; and it should be abated as a nuisance."

Like the churches in Kansas that kept being rebuilt, a third prison was constructed at Twentieth and Vine streets, just south of what would later become Kansas City's famous Eighteenth and Vine jazz district. It was made of stone, limestone in fact, with walls three feet thick. It would be a castlelike baronial structure with side and rear walls eighteen to twenty feet high. The building was inspired by western European castles from the Middle Ages. A steam fan system pumped heat into the cell rooms, one of the first known uses of forced ventilated air inside a pubic building. It stands there today, a mummy of its old self, much of the rock covered in ivy.

The workhouse started taking in prisoners in 1897. The city boasted that escape was practically impossible given the guards patrolling the grounds. Any prisoner daring enough to make a break for it would have to be, the city announced, "a second Monte Cristo."

Within eight years this third jail was as bad as the one it had replaced, filled with out-of-work paperhangers and roofers and day laborers who drank too much and could not pay their fines. Out front in the circle drive guards planted a DANGER sign, warning that "positively no parking" was allowed. They raised a U.S. flag from atop the highest turret. A women's wing housed prostitutes.

But it was not always impregnable, and inmates were keen on searching out escape routes. On June 22, 1908, a week after my grandfather was born, Ada Parker, twenty-three years old, described as "fat and dissatisfied with her environment," spotted a hole in a floor made by plumbers. Soon after midnight she sneaked out of bed with her blankets and sheets. She tied them together and lowered herself down the hole. But she landed in the prison pantry, crashing on top of the workhouse china, glassware, and tin pans. The ruckus woke up the guards. Ada was cut and bleeding, and the workhouse surgeon, Dr. George R. Dagg, patched her up. The next day the plumbers patched up the hole.

For the men it was a workhouse, plain and simple. Each morning they were shackled together and marched out to a stone pile. Other inmates hauled the crushed rock to road crews paving new streets. After an hour for lunch and a second afternoon shift back at the rock pile, the prisoners were lockstepped into their cells. By six in the evening it was lights out.

Many were desperate for freedom. Any means would do. Otto Rivers, an opium addict at twenty-seven, had served three months when in September 1907 he overpowered the head guard, John Spangler. He wrestled Spangler's revolver from his hip pocket and accidentally shot and wounded the guard. Rivers did not mean to shoot him. He meant to shoot himself. Twice earlier that day he had tried to kill himself. He set his bunk on fire but lost the nerve to let the flames reach him on the bed. He shattered a two-ounce bottle and started to swallow the broken glass. A police ambulance was summoned, and Rivers was about to leave for the city hospital when he lunged for the guard's weapon.

Another man wanted out so bad that he tried to claim insanity, even as a city commission blamed his troubles on "temper and booze." Jack Gallagher, described as a "notorious circumventor of justice," was serving a one-year sentence. He appealed to the city lunacy commission. During the hearing he kept dropping his eyes and nervously moving his hands and feet. Commission members saw it all as an act.

Gallagher testified that he had once been in the saloon business but lost his place, and that had led to his fits of anxiety. He lost weight, fought with a friend who beat him with a cane, and now he had trouble remembering certain things.

"Is your memory good?" asked Dr. St. Elmo Saunders.

"Yes," Gallagher blurted out, then looked nervously about the room. Well, he said, "there have been times when I have overlooked my mail for a day or two, but they were mostly bills."

A lawyer, J. F. Richardson, got to the point. "Do you drink intoxicating liquor?" he asked Gallagher.

"Yes."

"Do you ever get drunk?"

"Yes. I have drank whiskey ever since I was 20 years old. . . . I drink every day from 60 to 75 glasses of whiskey."

Police captain Frank Snow was called to the stand. He had known Gallagher for ten or fifteen years, mostly around the Fifth and Main area. "Do you think Jack is insane?" the police captain was asked.

"No," he testified. "Jack would not have any trouble if he would let the booze alone. Every man, or almost every man, who has owned a saloon on East Fourth Street has gone crazy and Jack will go the same way if he keeps up his present pace."

Back to the rock pile went Jack Gallagher.

But by June 1911 the workhouse days were numbered. To replace it, the city approved fifty thousand dollars in bonds to construct a "house of corrections" out on a high hill with 134 acres southeast of town in the old Leeds district.

The plan for the Kansas City Municipal Farm was borrowed from Cleveland, Ohio, which had a city farm system that taught skills to prisoners "so that upon their release, they could more easily locate some employment and avoid returning to prison again." Kansas City officials spent several days in Cleveland, impressed with this new prison-reform movement. "There are more than 130 acres of beautiful rolling land" out in Leeds, they said in a joint statement after returning home. They were eager to replace the stone walls of the city workhouse with fields and fruit orchards. "The prisoner coming from the smoke, grime and degradation of the city cannot help being uplifted by healthful work to take his mind off his troubles, fresh air to breathe and a good county diet. If the Farm can bring out the original manhood of which every prisoner has left at least a little, it will be a success."

So proud were Kansas City officials that in 1924 the Board of Public Welfare printed up a flyer with a picture of their new prison Farm touting how agriculture and gardening and other pursuits, like the quarry and the dairy and hog tending, were going to save the day. And it would rescue some lost souls, too, they promised. "Here drug addicts are treated and cured," the city proclaimed. "Under this plan men are released in good physical condition, cured of diseases and of the liquor habit and drug addiction and able to face the world in a manner worthy of citizenship."

The Farm when it opened was described as one of the "conspicuous successes" of the welfare movement. High praise, if seldom true.

To build it the city started trucking the prisoners from the old Vine Street workhouse out to Leeds. They housed them in a stockade and in tents on the Farm grounds and made them start clearing the brush. Guards began hoisting sawed-off shotguns to keep the prisoners in line rather than the old revolvers carried by officers at the workhouse.

When they started burying paupers nearby, they supervised that, too. "The guards would stand up on top of the hill with their shotguns and watch us the whole time," recalled grave digger Arthur Jones. "Some of the men were pretty superstitious and would hardly be able to move they were so scared of the bodies."

It took them nine years to finish the new facility, and W. H. Mc-Cracken could hardly wait to get the doors opened. He and others believed fresh air and hard work would go a long way to reform the city's miscreants. It would bring in city revenue, too, they said. Why, the mayor added, "yesterday I took the responsibility of paroling a man because he had work to go to and his children were suffering."

But Leeds, the area where they chose to put the Farm, was haunted. Everyone knew that. It was ghostly Blue River bottomland, and in Leeds all sorts of strange and unexplainable occurrences were known to happen. Leeds was bewitched, and in hindsight the city might have chosen a better location to put a working prison than on a hill and in the ground thousands of poor dead people nobody had ever wanted or anyone ever claimed.

One brisk morning in March 1920, just as the jail was being completed, a farmer near the new prison grounds heard a squawking noise in his chicken house. H. W. Storms went out to investigate, creeping in the darkness with his pistol in hand, just in time to make out a man running from the coop. Storms was a good shot, and he fired three times.

The prowler identified himself to police as John Jones. He said he was thirty-five years old and came from Girard, Kansas. But police could not match him with anyone with that name from Girard. They took him to the city hospital, as he was, they said, "wounded dangerously."

The man lingered for two weeks. Farmer Storms had not missed a shot, and the chicken thief's three wounds to the side, arm, and abdomen never healed. He died, and no one claimed his body. All police could find was a large undisclosed sum of money in his pockets. They kept his body on ice for another two weeks and they waited, and still no relatives stepped forward. Whoever he really was, no tongue could tell.

A few years earlier there rose the mystery of the bundled clothing. Some girls' apparel was found under a Leeds bridge, and local residents thought it probably belonged to what they suspected was a "gypsy" family camped nearby. Carl Cramer, a paperhanger, was the one who discovered the clothes, and he quickly spread the rumor. Soon all of Leeds was in an uproar. Probably murder or suicide, everyone guessed.

But the "gypsies" were talked to, and the girls too, with the whole family sitting around an outdoor campfire in front of their tent. The father denied he was a gypsy at all; he said he hailed from Pierce City, Missouri, and that he was a farmer. He was scantily clothed, though, and he had this long white beard. The whole family was in rags, and they had little to eat. The girls, Myrtle and Mabel, fourteen and ten years old, denied the clothes under the bridge were theirs, though they sure could have used a new dress or a pair of shoes. Nobody knew what to do next, except take the bundle of clothes and store it in Albert Witte's saloon in Leeds "for future reference."

The hamlet of Leeds was tiny and spare. It once was called "Alleytown" because its few streets were not named streets at all, just alleys up and down the neighborhood. One day Arthur Twitty, a patient at the city hospital in Kansas City, gave everyone a fright when he came walking through Leeds. He was demented, they said. He had wandered away from the hospital, caught the Belt Line train, and hopped off at Leeds. He plopped himself under a tree in the yard of Miss Sallie Lane and promptly drew stares because of the large bandage covering his head. To chase the gawkers away, Twitty snarled and said he was a leper. That certainly sent everyone a-scurrying.

For years the area was filled with sheep pens, and it was not until the mid-1920s that the first water mains were laid. That meant indoor toilets and improved fire protection. A few years after that Chevrolet built a large plant in Leeds, and my father worked there for years.

Yes, some things were coming up in Leeds, but others were going down. For years a sink hole in the ground kept growing larger and larger, and it finally consumed a two-story, five-room house that had belonged to the George Hillson family. All five of the Hillson children had been born in that house, and now their home lay bottom-up in this giant sink hole. Some speculated that mining operations in the old days might have loosened the earth around Leeds. Other said it was from aftershocks from a long-ago earthquake. Unsettled ground, they said. There were just a lot of things in Leeds that nobody could explain.

My grandfather's death would be one of them.

In time his prison would manage one of the largest pig-farm operations in the nation. That was the whole idea, to make the Farm pay for itself through prison labor and hope that hard work would rehabilitate men's lives. A noble idea, but impractical. For many inmates, the hog pens and the stables and the quarry and even for a while a facility that made rat bait from chicken feed and peanut oil—they were all just a revolving door. Prisoners came and they went and came back, usually for short stays. Nobody ever stayed long enough to die there, not yet anyway. A drunk named Sam passed through 143 times. Other inmates reached the point where they stopped counting—Joe Savershnick in and out of jail 121 times, Tony Magness 90 times, Ollie Watkins 61 trips to the Kansas City Municipal Farm. But the city was determined to make a go of it, to save lives and to save taxpayer money.

The pigs were fed garbage collected by city garbage trucks. Chickens raised by inmates were sold to local restaurants, including Stroud's. The Farm boasted a sawmill with logs supplied free from the city Park Department, making a handsome profit when the lumber was sold. If inmates worked hard and behaved and the guards were in a good mood, the prisoners ate in the mess hall, often dining on the very corn and vegetables that they raised right there.

But all was not pastoral. Life at the Municipal Farm soon would come under the same kind of public criticism leveled at the old workhouse. Conditions there could be just as harsh as at Twentieth and Vine. So bad were things that investigators were forced to announce that records in the Welfare Department were missing, that for a time there were no copies of paid invoices or even a list of vehicles in the Farm fleet. One Farm employee testified that most of the prison records "were taken out and destroyed by the superintendent."

I went out to the Farm looking for records from 1948 and particularly the files on my grandfather. The Castle was no more; in its

place stood a smaller modern facility. Most of the Farm's outbuild-
ings, like its fields, had been plowed under.

Nancy Leazer, the superintendent of corrections, was fascinated
with my hunt for my grandfather. A gracious woman, she shared
old photographs of the Farm operation and a short history of the
Castle. But she had no records of 1948 and no files on inmate James
Lyons. She did not even know that a man had died there.

Then Leazer remembered an old metal pig shed out in a heavily
wooded section of the property. We drove there on a curving, rutted
gravel lane. The barn seemed the size of a football field, low slung,
built of concrete and tin, nail-studded ply board strewn about. A
watchman met us, but he had bad news. Teenage vandals had just
broken in through the windows.

Bravely, we stepped inside and there found a room littered with
ripped-open boxes and files scattered about the shelves and floor.
Paper waist high filled the cavernous room. Much of it was water-
damaged, and the room stunk from mildew. Yet for what seemed
like several hours I pored through the heaps and the boxes, and
when I left the watchman bolted the door with a new lock and a
fresh chain and promised to return to hammer steel bars over the
windows. The oldest records I could find dated to the early 1970s.

Leazer's predecessor as warden was Cyriel Provyn, and he came
aboard in 1941. He stayed and ran the place until he retired in 1971.
He grew up in Belgium, and moved to Kansas City with his mother,
Emma. They were supposed to have sailed on the *Titanic* in 1912,
but they either arrived too late or the unsinkable wonder was already sold out. They took the next boat.

He and his mother cleared customs in New York, and soon they
joined his father in Kansas City down on the East Bottoms. In Belgium the family had lived in a fine, comfortable brick home. They
lived so well that his mother put beer in Cyriel's lunch thermos because she did not trust the local water at school. But in the East Bottoms, Emma Provyn wept when she saw the small river farm that
was now their home. It was nothing at all as spacious or as grand as
the large beautiful brick house they had left in the Old Country.

To the young boy it was Eden. In America everyone called him
"Cy," and he learned truck farming and row crops and eventually
spread out into the then vast farm fields of Kansas City, Kansas, and
beyond. His specialty was onions.

"He really knew how to farm and make a farm work," his nephew, John Nickerson, told me. "How to raise pigs. He got them in the pig business real good. The city was making money out of all that. He was quite a guy, you know. A good old boy. Six foot, kind of heavy, real likable."

Provyn would say later that when he first came out to the Farm he was appalled by all the squalor. Inmates slept on iron-grilled beds with haystacks and gunny sacks for mattresses. No sheets or blankets or pillows for the prisoners, either. Nobody worked, and every guard was armed. "You had to have a gun or a club to make your way into that kitchen," Provyn would recall in a 1951 interview. "The prisoners weren't given any work to do. They spent most of their time lying around upstairs. They had nothing to do, only sit around and get sick of themselves and their cellmates. I've seen two or three fights going on at once."

Provyn liked to say he was brought in because of his expertise as a farmer. But he would also admit that he had been hired for the job through the graces of the old Pendergast machine in Kansas City. "I paid my lugs and my cuts and put my money into the Christmas baskets," he said of payoffs to the boss. "I'll say this—I tried to get away from the machine but there weren't any other jobs. But I wouldn't have stayed with them much longer. I wasn't brought up that way."

Until he arrived, he said, the city had "never made a dime" off the Farm. He would change all that. He forced the prisoners out in the open air and into the fields, and soon there were mattresses and box springs and food served cafeteria-style in the mess hall. "It's been so long since we had a fight that I don't remember when the last one was," he boasted in that 1951 interview.

I guess he had already forgotten how just three years earlier my grandfather was covered with cuts and bruises and his neck was broken, and how he had been fed bread and water in the Hole instead of any cafeteria lunch. I guess he forgot too how the routine was bread and water for two days and then something else to chew on after that. But James Lyons did not make it that long in the Hole or the Dungeon, as the guards called it. He lasted just an hour and a day. And it could get cold down there, too, even in May. Some of the inmates were put in solitary confinement without any clothes to wear. They went into the Hole naked. Or in just their shorts.

Warden Provyn must have forgotten another fight as well, this one just a year after my grandfather's death, when he himself "scuffled" with an inmate and one of his senior guards was shot.

John Stapleton was a twenty-three-year-old prisoner in for sixty days for larceny. More precisely, he was a hat thief, caught carrying several hats near a millinery shop that had been looted. After two weeks at the Farm he escaped into the woods while working on an afternoon brush-cutting detail. Provyn and the guard, Estel Long, took off after him in one of the Farm cars, with the warden behind the wheel. Provyn had brought his gun, and they spotted Stapleton walking near U.S. Highway 50.

Provyn stepped out, aimed the gun at the escapee, and ordered him into the back of the car with Officer Long. But Stapleton did not want to go back to that jail. He started to move like he was going to oblige but then quickly lunged for Provyn's revolver. In the struggle the weapon fired just as Long was jumping out to help the warden. The guard took the bullet in his right foot—right between the toes.

No one wanted to go back there. Many thought the Farm an old devil's place, just like they said Leeds was haunted. There even was an old jailhouse blues song out at the Farm that many prisoners knew by heart. It went about like this:

> Well, I'm sitting here in Leeds Farm
> And I really don't give a damn
> They brought me up in a pickup truck
> And handcuffed both my hands.
>
> Well, they took all my clothes
> And they took all my dough
> And hell they took my underwear
> Now I'm sittin' here writin' this song
> With those green Leeds underwear
> Blues.

But it was the chorus that really hit home when I thought about my grandfather, after first hearing the song. I was working then as a city desk editor on the *Kansas City Times,* and one of our columnists brought a copy of the lyrics into the newsroom. The chorus went like this:

I ain't really good
And I ain't really bad
That goes for all my friends too.

Yet much of the public was fooled into thinking life on the Farm was just rolling along, that things were idyllic out in Leeds. In March 1948, two months before my grandfather arrived, the *Star* called the prison a "model" institution. "There are a canteen, a recreation program, religious services, medical and dental care, and a reading and music room for relaxation. Many of the prisoners ask for some particular phase of the work program and their requests are granted as far as possible."

On May 1948, just days before my grandfather died there, the newspaper said the city ran an "ideal farm." Most of the credit went to Provyn. "The group of men who arrives at the Farm each day does not resemble a group of farm hands," the paper said. "There are long beards and bleary eyes and cuts and bruises, for many of the men bear the scars of fights and falls. These men are examined by physicians, cleaned up, given clothes and shaves and hair cuts. Soon they are farm hands with shovels or other implements in their hands, or driving tractors or mules."

In truth the Kansas City Municipal Farm could be a horrendous place, and it remained so even after my grandfather died there and into the years beyond. In 1950 a Community Studies group toured the facility and complained how closely the inmates were locked down under the threat of armed guards. But this was supposed to be a minimum-security institution, so why were "most of the men working in gangs under guard"? The visiting community group said that "with this type of prisoners it is neither necessary nor desirable to have super security facilities such as are found at institutions like the federal prison at Alcatraz."

Most were drunks unable to pay their fines. My grandfather was one of the 460 drunks taken out there in May 1948, a steady increase over previous years. In the whole prison, drunkenness accounted for nearly 60 percent of all the inmate commitments. "That a large number of these people must do time is merely their hard luck in not having enough money to pay the fine," the group said.

The prison by then was at its heaviest population load over the previous ten years, and the Community Studies panel called for

more rehabilitation programs for alcoholics other than straight prison time. Along with it the group wanted a "city-wide drive against
overindulgence in alcohol." They also wanted the building remod-
eled, toilets upgraded, and water and sanitary pipes "replaced
throughout." These were not violent prisoners. Take down the iron
bars and put up wooden doors on the cells.

None of the improvements were implemented. Instead, there followed a long series of blistering Jackson County Grand Jury investigations, as jurors repeatedly drove out to the Leeds facility and
took their own look around, inspecting the Castle building and the
Farm grounds and operations. They always came away unhappy
with what they saw.

The first was in September 1952 when grand jurors sharply criti-
cized "overcrowded conditions" at the jail. "The mess hall, benches,
floor and kitchen were unsanitary. This institution is badly overcrowded, lacks toilet facilities and there is a serious fire hazard."

The next inspection was conducted two years later. "We found a
deplorable, unsanitary, shocking and inhuman condition existing at
the Municipal Farm," grand jurors said. "The Farm was built for a
capacity of 180 inmates and at the present time there are 332 confined
there, which make the living conditions intolerable. As many as 91
men were sleeping in one ward, with their toilet facilities limited to
two stools. There was a complete lack of showers and kitchen facilities; no recreation space of any type or description. In general, conditions were so bad," the grand jurors said, that they recommended a
bond issue to tear down the Castle building and start all over again.
"The present facilities could not possibly be rehabilitated."

A follow-up grand jury three months later found no improvements and instead identified "230 inmates confined and living under
very severe conditions with a lack of sanitary facilities, kitchen and
food handling facilities, recreation and supervision facilities. It is
our opinion that it would be impossible to attempt to utilize the
present buildings in any new program."

Two months later and the grand jury still was not pleased: "The
buildings under the present overcrowded condition are entirely inadequate. Immediate consideration should be given to the construction of a new penal building for men."

Still the city did little and the prison Farm grew worse, and more
inmates were piled in and more became desperate to get out. In 1965,

five prisoners cut through a second-floor window and made off. Provyn said it was not the guards' fault; it was just that the prison had been designed poorly. "It apparently took them some time," he said. "They had to cut through the tops and bottoms of three bars, all hardened steel, and then cut once through a cross bar." He said the corner of the cell block could not be watched by a guard. Then conceding that conditions indeed were pretty bad in his prison, the warden added, "The guard can't walk in there at night with any safety."

A year later members of the city council went out to Leeds for their own look around. They found the crumbling Castle holding twice the number of inmates it was designed for. Beds were packed in close and tight, in cell blocks, recreation rooms, and hallways. Prisoners sat on the stairs, in the doorways, and in the halls. Some of the beds were bare, and some of the men had no shirts to wear. "This is the one thing I am ashamed of in my city," said city manager Carleton Sharpe. Mayor Ilus W. Davis agreed. "This is no credit to the city," he said.

The Municipal Farm now was nearly fifty years old, and the next month, August 1966, the city council voted to launch plans for a new city jail in Leeds. It passed unanimously except for one dissenter, councilwoman Mrs. Harry Hagan. She represented the Leeds district, and she said Leeds did not want the prison anymore.

The building kept crumbling, and inmates kept running off. Things were so lax that in September 1970, just months before the old building came down and a new one started up, two inmates hopped off a work truck in the center of the city and disappeared. The guard, Stephen Lee, did not even know they were gone until "I was clear back to the Farm." The escapees, Jack Townsen and Lonnie Newell, vanished in their green prison uniforms. Both were older men, and both were drunks.

Finally, it was not until the end of the 1970s that the "bread and water diet" officially was erased from the books at city hall. But even at that late date, James D. H. Reefer, then the city community services director, could not recall the last time that any prisoner went hungry because he needed a little "straightening out." Reefer also did not know when "isolation cells" last were used. But he noted that they had long served as extra punishment and that inmates "still could face the threat of solitary confinement."

Gone now were the old days, the times when Cy Provyn for as long as he ran the place lived alone in the warden's little white house on the Farm, sitting there on his porch and watching over his prison acreage. Several of his top jail lieutenants and their young families lived there, too. But it was the warden who knew how to handle just about any job on the Farm, and Provyn made clear that he was the boss. Sometimes when the day was done he would relax on his porch there and think up more chores for the morning. Farming was in his blood. He was a farmer first and a warden second.

John Noble, the only guard I could find still living, and he retired in 1991 after more than twenty-five years there, had vivid memories of Provyn and his never-ending tasks to keep the Farm running. There was the animal shelter and the chicken coops that had to be cleaned and the large asparagus beds to be tended. For a while they baked their own pies. "And we produced a lot of tomatoes," Noble said.

The worst thing he said ever happened while he was there was an altercation between a guard and a prisoner out in the fields. "An officer, a new one, was on a detail and they were working with shovels, and the officer hit one of the inmates right across the face with the blade of one of the shovels," Noble said. "I don't remember if he died or not."

Noble came to the Farm in 1964, long after my grandfather died, and he swore he never heard of the incident when I found him in retirement up in St. Joseph, Missouri. He did remember the Hole, though, and how before his time at the jail prisoners put in solitary were fed bread and water. One day he peered into the Hole, long after it had been emptied out and was no longer in use. "But I couldn't see into it very well," he told me. "It was too dark." He did not dare step in.

Harvey Porch ran the Farm cannery and laundry operation. He and his wife, Nancy, were raising three small boys, and she really did not want to move out there. But she came to like the place soon enough. So did her sons.

"The inmates were wonderful to the boys," Nancy recalled. "They didn't cuss around them. They would tell them why they were there, though, and would tell them, 'Don't you go bad.' If they had school problems, they'd help. One boy had to make a model house, and an inmate was a carpenter by trade."

Provyn, she said, "had heart" for the inmates, many of them drunks suffering from delirium tremens when they first set foot under the archway out front. The prisoners were unloaded right there, quite often unsteady on their feet, escorted out of a large jail bus that the staff called the Blue Goose.

"He was strict with them," she said of Warden Provyn's attitude toward his charges. "They couldn't just slack off. They usually had the d.t.'s at first, and they'd get out to the Farm around right after lunch, and the next morning they were out on a work detail. They might not be able to work, but they were out in the fresh air. They made the men get out in the fresh air right away."

There was no breathable air in the Hole, not even a breeze, certainly not a window, and Nancy Porch never cared to see it. But she did remember hearing of the dark, cold basement cell below the Castle walls. "The prisoners really didn't want to go down there. But they warned them ahead of time. If you didn't behave, that's where you're going to go. Harvey talked about the Hole and how they tried their best not to have to put people down there."

The children of guards living on the Farm said it gave them a glorious childhood. Patricia Plagge, whose father worked as head jail mechanic, can still recall delightful summer days on the vast property. It was especially magical for her as a young preschooler. Nothing upset her. "They weren't bad people. They didn't scare me," she said of the inmates. "But I also remember when some were trying to escape and running down the woods. We had a dog. He was part beagle and he had a good nose, and the guards would swing by with flashlights and grab our dog and set after them."

Her brother, Mike Kliethermes, can also still see the fleeing escapees. He can still envision them taking off down the hill, slipping away with the big bright letters *MF* for "Municipal Farm" sewn into the backs of their prison khakis. He did not blame them for running. "They would walk off all the time," he said. "They would go out in the fields and hoe and whatever else they were told to do. Twenty-five would go out, and twenty-four would come back. Those that left always started walking toward town. They'd go home and see their wife, and they'd go out the next morning and were brought back."

He recalled playing around the headstones at the pauper's cemetery. One of the headstones was in a field right in front of their house on the Farm grounds. Kliethermes also remembered running carefree through the Castle, first through a garage entrance and then around the boiler room, up and down a passageway and into the kitchen and mess hall, grabbing something to eat before heading upstairs and into "a big room full of a whole bunch of beds." He said, "I never worried about anything being over there. The prisoners got a warm place to sleep and free meals. There were some guys who were always there. They'd get out and they'd be right back."

The warden watched over both guards and prisoners alike. His nephew, John Nickerson, told me that his other uncle, Ben Provyn, was always being arrested by the police and trotted out to the Farm. There, Warden Provyn would check the daily bed count each morning, and whenever he found his brother on the list he made sure to set him free. "He was like a lot of the gandies back then," Nickerson said of his uncle Ben. "He was harmless. But he used to get hold of that wine, and he'd lost an eye working on the railroad. He'd get paychecks every now and then to cover that, and then he'd get to drinking. As soon as he hit the Farm, Uncle Cyriel would see his name on the register, and he'd have to get him out of there. Didn't want him in there."

On Sundays Nickerson and his mother would visit the Farm, and Warden Provyn loaded them up with chickens plucked and ready to fry. He would send them home with big ripe tomatoes and ears of corn and a basket full of onions, of course. When he was in high school Nickerson would ride his bicycle out to the Farm on long summer afternoons. He would tag around with his uncle and eat lunch with the guards. "This was around 1945 and 1946," he told me. "Most of the prisoners, you couldn't say they were hard-core. A lot of them were probably winos and small-time thieves. And I remember they had what the inmates called the Hole. They'd stick a guy in the Hole a couple of days. You'd shut the door and it got real dark in there. They got water and probably a little food. It was just this cell in the basement. I remember one time to scare me they put me in there and shut the door. So I could feel what it was like. It was black dark, and I couldn't even see my hand. All I could make out was a bucket in there."

Headline, *Kansas City News-Press*, May 1948. (Author's collection)

The Kansas City Municipal Farm, main building, also known as the Castle. (courtesy City of Kansas City)

A crumbling Kansas City Municipal Farm main building. (courtesy City of Kansas City)

An abandoned cell block at the Farm. (courtesy City of Kansas City)

Kansas City Municipal Farm cell. (courtesy City of Kansas City)

The old city jail, known as the workhouse. (courtesy *Kansas City Star*)

Cell block at the Kansas City Municipal Farm. (courtesy City of Kansas City)

My grandfather's parents, Irish immigrants Joseph and Mary Lyons (*right*). (Author's collection)

My grandfather's mother, Mary Lyons, in old age, an Irish immigrant who buried four children and her husband. (Author's collection)

The only photo of my grandparents Zillah and James Lyons (*the couple at right*), in November 1930, apparently on their wedding day. (Author's collection)

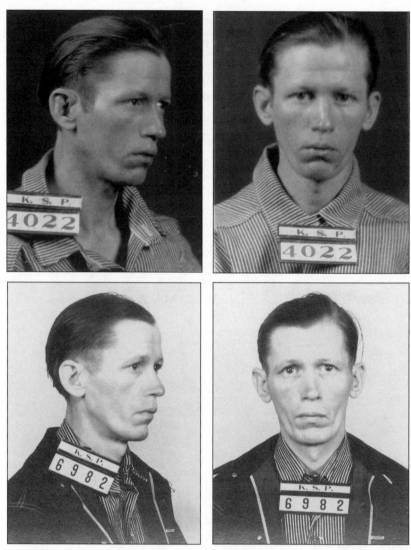

Kansas State Penitentiary mug shots of my grandfather's brother, Joseph P. Lyons Jr. (courtesy Kansas State Historical Society)

Kirby McRill, one of my grandfather's last roommates on skid row. (courtesy *Kansas City Star*)

Kansas City police officer Harry Nesbitt, my friend's fabled straight-shooting grandfather. (courtesy *Kansas City Star*)

My grandfather's last home, Fifth and Main streets—the city's skid row—in the late 1940s. (courtesy Missouri Valley Special Collections, Kansas City Public Library, Kansas City, Missouri)

Warden Cyriel Provyn for years oversaw the jail and grounds at the Kansas City Municipal Farm. (courtesy *Kansas City Star*)

Jackson County sheriff J. A. Purdome on the day he married his new bride, Esther, the widow of Wolf C. Rimann who was slain gangland-style in another never-solved homicide. (courtesy *Kansas City Star*)

CHAPTER 6

When the guard's spotlight landed on James Lyons the jail announced that officers had looked in on him several times down there in the Hole and that he seemed to be fine, and they suggested that even though he was not yet forty years old, he must have had a stroke or a heart attack or something. Nothing unusual, they said. But because the Farm was city property and the guards were city employees, everyone thought it best to turn the investigation over to the Jackson County Sheriff's Department. That way there could be no hint of a conflict of interest, no suggestion that every tip and every lead was not followed to get to the bottom of what caused the man's death.

For Jackson County sheriff J. A. Purdome, it could not have come at a more awkward time. A Democrat, Purdome was up for reelection that year, and nothing was going right. Someone had broken into the double-door safe in the sheriff's office at the courthouse and stolen $14,661.50 in checks and cash from a small metal box—money under the sheriff's care from the sale of tax-delinquent properties.

A year earlier someone dynamited another vault in the downtown courthouse, this one below the sheriff's office, and made off with ballots and other election material being stored as legal evidence in a massive vote-rigging case soon to go to trial. At the time four of Purdome's deputies were under indictment in the vote-fraud investigation. But when the ballots were stolen and Purdome and his staff could not find them, it meant only one thing—criminal charges against the deputies were going to have to be dismissed. In other words, they got off.

Nevertheless Purdome promised swift and thorough investigations into both break-ins. He pledged to find the money and to recover the ballots. "We are pushing this investigation with everything we have," the sheriff said. "We will let the chips fall where they may."

Witnesses were hooked up to polygraph machines, and several deputies were taken before a grand jury. Depositions were recorded and evidence collected. But no one was arrested in either case, and no one went to jail. No chips fell.

Purdome was Jackson County sheriff for eight years—from 1945 through 1952. He earlier had served briefly as county sheriff during another courthouse scandal in 1940. He worked his way up on two fronts, toiling as a deputy and then chief deputy sheriff under his predecessor, James L. Williams, and also, and more important, as a Democratic political operative. J. A. Purdome was a Pendergast man, and the machine took him far.

He also fancied himself something of a homicide sleuth, and on occasion would give detailed stories to true-crime magazines, the kind of popular pulp trades that filled the imagination before television and the Internet stifled it. In one piece titled "Double Death at Sugar Creek," Chief Deputy J. D. Purdome (they got his middle initial wrong) rode to the rescue of a stalled investigation into the body of a woman found among the bogs and the bullfrogs upside the Missouri River.

He worked hard to learn the cool swagger of the big-city detective. This line alone in the magazine story he must have just loved, where it said, "Purdome took a cigarette from his pocket and lit it thoughtfully." They ran his picture, too—his thinning black hair combed straight back, his piercing black eyes, and his cheeks already jowly. He had been born in Arkansas, and family members said he actually was named Purdom but that he added an e onto his last name to give himself a little savoir faire when he left the Ozarks for the bright lights of Kansas City.

The big lights did him in. The sheriff's throne in Jackson County, Missouri, has always been a cushy seat to settle into, and for decades it could be reached only through the old spoils system and political favoritism that pervaded Kansas City. It was like a musical chair, too, often up for grabs after one political scandal followed another.

Joseph Reddeford Walker was first to claim the prize when the sheriff's office was created in 1828. He was a lot more than just a sheriff, though. Over the years he worked as a trapper, an explorer, and a guide; he scouted for the cavalry, and he rustled horses, too. He had a long nose and a long beard, and he wore a large floppy hat.

He liked to deck himself out in full mountain gear with two watch-like cases draped around his neck. Inside the cases he kept a pair of compasses, and a tiny telescope.

Walker made his true mark farther west, around Santa Fe and Taos and California. He helped discover routes through the Yosemite Valley. He was a friend to the Indians, including the local Osage and Kansas tribes, and he often bargained and traded with them in order to secure safe passage for the coming wagon trains. He was one of the first to camp along the Great Salt Lake and to cross up and over the Sierra Nevada. He felt an earthquake and witnessed a meteor shower. His brothers were pretty famous, too. John fell at the Alamo, and Joel built the first brick house in Jackson County. Joel then started leading adventure seekers out to Oregon.

Sheriff Joseph Reddeford Walker also befriended a young Indian woman, a "squaw," he called her, and when the sheriff's portrait was painted the artist depicted her walking behind him while he sat on horseback. That was how she showed respect for her man. But her true gift was making moccasins, and she presented the artist, Alfred Miller of Baltimore, with a dozen pair. So from the very beginning the office of Jackson County Sheriff was delicate shoes to fill.

Purdome did not blaze any trails; his trails were opened for him. He started out in Kansas City as a deputy county license inspector and by the mid-1930s was appointed through the largesse of Tom Pendergast to the position of county deputy sheriff. In 1937 he had done such a good job they elevated him to chief deputy. And at the close of 1940, for a brief sixty days, he actually was sheriff.

It happened this way: The real sheriff was James L. Williams. He had moved to Kansas City in 1928, exactly one hundred years after Walker was installed as the first sheriff. But where Walker tamed mountains, Williams was shy and withdrawn. He was small with blue eyes and had once taught public speaking to high school kids in little Enid, Oklahoma. He also worked as an adjuster, settling insurance claims. But starting over in Kansas City he managed to slide in good with the Pendergast crowd and came to know another machine protégé, Harry Truman. Williams made his mark as a political-poll book carrier, tracking vote trends and then as a precinct captain. In 1936 they awarded him the sheriff's seat.

In later life he liked to reminisce to reporters about the good old days and how anyone with enough moxie could get ahead in Kansas City politics. "I learned right off that you had to involve yourself with the people of the community," Williams said. "Nobody in the 1930s had to tell us about what a state the United States was in. But we licked it by working together."

Things did not go well for Sheriff Williams. Six months after taking office he had to fire four deputies for taking bribes in return for releasing prisoners from the county jail on top of the downtown courthouse. By year's end two more deputies were fired for jury tampering, and also for selling jury summonses at a dollar apiece. It got worse. The next year several local attorneys revealed that deputies were demanding rake-off fees or else they would take their sweet time serving subpoenas. A sheriff's bookkeeper embezzled six thousand dollars in county funds for himself. Then things began to hit really close to home. The public started complaining that when sheriff's deputies were called to investigate minor traffic accidents, they always had the cars towed to a garage run by Sheriff Williams's brother.

And closer still: In 1940, when Williams was preparing to run for reelection, ouster proceedings were ordered by Governor Stark after evidence pointed to Williams taking thousands of dollars of federal money for housing federal prisoners in the county jail. In all he kept more than forty-six thousand dollars as personal "gravy." His jail books were a mess and it was hard for auditors to sort through them, but that was the grand total they reached. Then two dozen state liquor control inspectors were called to Kansas City to testify behind closed doors about saloon irregularities, including failure to enforce liquor and gambling laws.

Williams tried to hold things together. In his defense he said he had already refunded about sixteen thousand dollars of the money to the county. When the ouster report was released to the public and it called for his "immediate" removal, Williams tried to remain calm. He posed for news photographers wearing his trademark three-piece suit and lapel handkerchief. He crossed his legs and perused the report, and all the while he puffed on a big, thick cigar.

But Williams was gone. And in the confusion of that time, what the *Star* called "a dark chapter of official laxity matched by no other in the Pendergast hierarchy," J. A. Purdome ascended to the throne and was named to serve as temporary sheriff for the remaining two months of Williams's term. Purdome then went back to being the chief deputy.

But in 1944 he threw his own hat in the ring, as they liked to say back then, and was elected sheriff in his own right. One hundred deputies, many of them new hires handpicked by Purdome, were sworn in with him. When Purdome walked into the sheriff's office and took his seat at the desk he was greeted with six baskets of flowers from well-wishers. What could possibly go wrong?

Everything.

The public soon learned that not only was their new sheriff a product of the Pendergast operation, but he also was linked closely to Kansas City's underworld. As the top lawman in Jackson County he awarded honorary "deputy sheriff badges" to hoodlums around town who worked the tavern circuit. The most "honorable" was Wolf C. Rimann. His jukeboxes and slot machines were found in most of the local bars. He also held a hidden partnership in a good many of those taverns. He rose to prominence as a golf pro, and he lived life on the soft side until he was gunned down, shot to death in the middle of the afternoon. Rimann was killed in an ambush from a souped-up 1948 Ford that drew up real slow alongside him. He was hit in the shoulder, the neck, the head, and the leg.

Rimann's car was equipped with a special police siren and red lights, and a red-faced Purdome was forced to publicly admit that the gambling promoter was one of his special honorary deputies. The sheriff also had to concede that many nights when other squad cars were tied up, Rimann was permitted to play real cop and respond to the scenes of accidents and other emergencies. The sheriff had licensed him to carry a firearm, too.

To quiet growing public concerns, Purdome promised a thorough investigation of the Rimann murder. But the case withered down to a few slim clues and soon enough a dead end. No arrests here, either. Then before the year was out—surprise of surprises—the sheriff married Rimann's widow.

So in this election year of 1948 Purdome did not need any further aggravation or bad publicity from what looked like a jailhouse lynching in the basement cell of the Kansas City Municipal Farm. He was fighting for his political life that summer and would have wanted nothing more than for my grandfather's death to go away. He must have thought it a big nuisance. But things for Purdome with his underworld connections, his honorary badges, and his gangland widow turned a whole lot worse when a United States Senate committee investigating organized crime came to Kansas City and held a public hanging.

Senator Estes Kefauver of Tennessee, chairman of the Senate Crime Investigation Committee, was traveling the country targeting organized crime. He set up shop in the federal courthouse in downtown Kansas City in 1950, and panel members revisited the stolen county courthouse money and the ballots blasted out of the sheriff's vault. They discussed the tavern shakedowns, the slot machines, and the bullets fired into Wolf Rimann.

"Our job is not to solve crime, although we would be glad to do that if it should come out in any hearing," Kefauver said after arriving in Kansas City from Washington, D.C. "We do not try to supersede or interfere in what is primarily a local law enforcement matter." But he warned that the good people of Kansas City and Jackson County were being terrorized by a small knot of gangsters and crooked cops, and that his committee planned to expose them. "We know the overwhelming proportion of people here are fine, honest men and women who have been imposed upon by a very few men," the senator said.

He went to work at ten o'clock the next morning when the hearings opened in the courtroom of U.S. district judge Albert L. Reeves. For three days the room was filled to capacity, and each morning and afternoon the sessions blanketed the local papers and crowded the radio airwaves. It was like nothing the town had seen or heard or read before. When it was over, the *Star* editorialized that the public had come "face to face" with the underground and the dishonest cop, and that in the next election cycle it would be time for change. "The responsibility for action here is on the people of Kansas City. The citizen's weapon is his ballot."

One of the committee's first concerns was the number of unsolved murders that were adding up and the inability of law enforcement officials to make arrests. One of the first to testify was Kansas City police detective Lt. Harry Nesbitt. "People are scared to death," he told the committee.

Harry Nesbitt in a world of ironies was staring me down again. I instantly recognized him as the crime-busting, sharpshooting grandfather of my grade school friend Dave Nesbitt. Dave had the hero cop for a grandfather. I had the town drunk. I stumbled across the coincidence one Saturday afternoon in the beautiful Library of

Congress reading room, settling in under a desk light with bound books of transcripts from the Kefauver hearings.

Detective Lieutenant Nesbitt and two other high-ranking city police officials, clearly unhappy with the way Purdome was running the sheriff's department, testified that investigations into a string of spectacular and unsolved homicides had been seriously hampered not just by the intimidation of witnesses but also by links between the underworld and elements connected to the sheriff's sanctum. They had Rimann in mind. But they brought other names with them, too.

Nesbitt's pistol-packing days as a patrolman were over. He now headed up the city police homicide bureau, and he provided a roster of unsolved slayings from 1940 to 1950. Rimann, of course, topped the list. But also prominently displayed were two North End gangland leaders and political operatives, the "two Charlies," as they were known—Charles Binaggio and Charles Gargotta, killed together earlier that year in a political club on Truman Road. Their bodies were splayed out under a five-times-larger-than-life, get-out-the-vote portrait of hometown favorite Harry Truman. Truman was in the White House by then, and it made for a sensational photograph in the *Star* and splashed all across the nation. But sometimes such things are staged, and a rumor persisted for years around the newsroom that the photographer moved the picture on the wall so he could make a better shot. The bodies he let lie still.

Binaggio, Nesbitt told the committee, was a "prominent political leader and reportedly was involved in nationwide gambling operations." Gargotta, he said, "was a well-known gunman and muscleman engaged in gambling operations."

Also among the dead was one of Purdome's own deputies. Louis Cuccia was born in Brooklyn, New York, to parents who came from Italy. Eventually, they moved to Kansas City, and young Louis got himself a badge and went to work for Sheriff Purdome. In January 1946 he was sitting in a car in front of a liquor store on the city's Northeast Side. The car was a Pontiac, and it belonged to Nick Civella, who in ensuing years would rise to the helm of the Kansas City underworld, replacing the two Charlies. Why Deputy Cuccia was in Civella's car and what they were discussing can only be imagined. What happened next is what happened to Rimann. A car slowed up alongside them, and someone opened fire. The gunshots were clearly meant for Civella, but Cuccia took the hit. He was shot dead in the head. Neither Civella nor the killers nor anyone else was held accountable. Cuccia was forty-three years old. He used to be a barber, and that deputy's job meant the world to him. Civella was thirty-five. He worked at the Truckers Liquor Market, but what he really did was provide muscle for the mob.

"The first shot threw glass in my face and blinded me," Civella told police investigators, explaining why he could not make out the assailants. "I then ducked down and opened the door and fell out onto the sidewalk," he said, explaining further why he did not see the faces of the driver or the triggerman with the Thompson submachine gun. "I looked up and saw a dark colored car with two tail lights going east on Fifteenth. I didn't see the occupants."

Sheriff Purdome was incensed that one of his own had been murdered. Heads are going to roll, he said. "This will be the last of this for awhile," he declared. "I'm going to put deputies to patrolling the streets inside the city and put a stop to this foolishness. We're not going to stop until this thing is solved. But whatever the cause for this slaying might be, the men made two mistakes. They killed the wrong man and they killed a deputy sheriff."

What really turned out to be foolish were Purdome's remarks because no one was pinned to the slaying. Instead, it became just another murder on the long list of unsolved homicides that were presented to the Kefauver committee. The list also included those far less recognizable, the far less notorious, the simple, the plain, men and women, black and white, their names one after another read out to the committee.

On April 12, 1940, Mrs. Ruth H. Harding was found in an alley garage at the rear of 1420 Olive. She had apparently been raped and beaten to death. A blow over her right eye fractured her skull. She was attacked while returning home from the movies. No one saw anything, but a dog would not stop barking. Police noted her black coat was disheveled and her black straw hat knocked off her head. She died a block from her home, her body discovered by a young man walking through the alley who noticed the garage doors slightly ajar. He peeked inside and found her lying atop a pile of coal.

Other unsolved cases involved low-level hoods. John Mutolo, known to all as "Johnny Mutt," was shot on a felt-covered card table at the Eleventh Ward Democratic Club at 608 Brooklyn Avenue. He was a well-known police character and petty gambler. He was thirty-two, a burglar and a three-time ex-con, and he was killed on October 6, 1947. He was sleeping on the table when they got him. Someone had made a three-rung homemade ladder out of rope and planks and scurried up the side of the building to peer inside. The window was raised four inches, just enough to slide a shotgun barrel through, and Johnny Mutt was hit by several blasts in the back. Police found four empty beer bottles, a pop bottle, and two playing cards on the ground near the ladder, clues the gunman waited for Johnny to nod off. He had been arrested forty-two times and last left the Missouri State Penitentiary nine months before his death. His family told police they knew no one who had it in for him, but his wife said he had recently told her, "Someone is going to be killed and I probably will be next."

A month before my grandfather died, Mike Licausi was shot in front of the Second Ward Democratic Club at 1017 East Fifteenth Street. It actually was a front for a gambling joint, and Licausi had a share in the take. In 1939 he was sent away on federal drug charges, including selling heroin, and for that he was known as a "big man" in the local rackets. He was slain early in the morning after stepping out of the club with a friend. A double blast from a 12-gauge shotgun put him down. Police interviewed the dice men and cardsharps, and they said Licausi had been having a tough go of it. He had been losing at the tables, and he was borrowing money to keep the game afloat. His partner, William M. Lowman, a former Jackson County deputy sheriff, left early that night because things were too quiet. Not enough action, he said. "Mike said it was getting a little dull and suggested that we fold," Lowman told police. And so they folded.

Nesbitt and his fellow police commanders were not blaming so many open homicide investigations on Purdome's sheriff's office. But the implication was there—that Purdome's crew was either unwilling or unable to put a murder case together, in a city with a dangerously spreading criminal culture, one that frightened witnesses and allowed crime to go unchecked. The fact that his deputies were ill-equipped or simply looked the other way did nothing to encourage witnesses to step forward. "People are scared to death," Nesbitt said.

His colleague police detective Lt. Clarence S. Raisbeck testified about the stolen ballots. "We found the vault had been forced open and three sealed ballot boxes had been forced open and the ballots taken," Raisbeck testified. "All the members of the burglary bureau, which consisted of about 25 people, were assigned to the investigation. We enlisted the cooperation of the sheriff in every way."

He said the FBI was called in and the county prosecutor, too, James Kimbrell. But the case went nowhere. "No solution to the burglary has been determined," Raisbeck said. "It was later found that the safe had been blown open by the use of an explosive, which was unnecessary to get the door open. It could have been opened very easily without explosives."

By that he seemed to be hinting the theft was an inside job, suggesting that bombing open the safe might have been a ruse to make the public think it was someone other than a deputy who would have known the combination. "It was not a vault door as we understand a vault," he said. "What I mean, it was just a light steel door with a combination lock, like a safe. It was very light, very flimsy. It is a record cabinet is what it is, built in there as a record cabinet and not as a vault."

Kefauver asked him, "It could have been pried open with a crow bar?"

"That is right."

The panel quizzed another of Nesbitt's city police colleagues, Lt. Charles J. Welch, about the Rimann murder. He told about the drive-by shooting and the jukebox and slot—machine kingpin lying facedown on the cushion of his car, his feet barely touching the pavement. "He had been shot five times," Welch said.

He described witness accounts of possibly two men in the rear of the passing car, how bullets echoed on the street and the coup de grâce at a quarter to three in the afternoon, on the corner of Fourteenth and Chestnut streets. "There was a shot fired from the killers' car in the direction of Mr. Rimann's car," Welch said. "In our opinion that first shot hit the windshield of Mr. Rimann's car. The man on the left or west side of this killer car got out, went over to Mr. Rimann, who was getting into his car, and fired several shots into his body."

The second gunman in the "killer car," a black Ford sedan, hopped out, too. He scurried behind the Ford and made sure no one interfered. He had to scurry to make it back in the Ford as it sped off.

The car was recovered at Twenty-sixth and Smart streets. A crew took it to the police garage, and they began processing the vehicle. "There were two gun cases found concealed in the car, one of them

under the footrest in the back seat, and which would hold possibly three to four side arms," Welch told the panel. "This car was
lined with red leather. It appeared to be very new. In the backrest
of the back seat, there was found another gun case. That was large
enough to hold a machine gun or sawed off shotguns. This was
welded to the springs of the car of the back seat, and it was also
lined with red leather."

Rimann's car was outfitted nicely to complement his status as an
honorary deputy sheriff, so honored by Sheriff J. A. Purdome. "It is
my understanding," Welch told an astonished Kefauver committee,
"that he was a deputy sheriff, held a commission as a deputy sheriff."

At the time he was gunned down the forty-three-year-old Rimann
had just obtained a statewide liquor license. He was reportedly
planning to expand his operations into the wholesale whiskey business. He already ran the local Hillcrest Country Club, which was
described by police as his "surface activity"—that is, his cover to
make him look legit. Just an hour before he was killed there had
been a final bank conference to put him in position to take over the
wholesale whiskey distributorship for western Missouri and large
swaths of Kansas. He was said to have a financial net worth of half
a million dollars, no small amount for 1948. Rimann when he died
was on the threshold of big business deals; he was about to begin
piling up real dollars. He was so flush with cash that Rimann and
his wife, Esther, and their son lived in high style out at the club.
They recently had vacationed in Mexico.

Even on his last day he was quite the busy man. He had coffee
with a woman friend. He deposited seventeen hundred dollars in a
bank and negotiated a twenty thousand–dollar loan at another. He
discussed some previous threats on his life with the man who ran his
coin-machine operation. He picked up some clothes and dropped
by an upholstery company to see about getting a few chairs redone.
Then he stepped out one last time—toward his car.

"He was happy as he always was," Esther Rimann, his wife-
turned-widow, told reporters after he died. He had drawn up a will
three years earlier, and she, as his wife, was the main beneficiary.

Immediately, Purdome was besieged by reporters. He tried to
explain away why Rimann was given a special deputy commission and a police siren, saying Rimann was a member of the sheriff's mounted horse patrol and had participated in ceremonies for

President Truman's inauguration. Purdome said Rimann actually on occasion responded to police calls, such as traffic accidents. Purdome knew Rimann so well, he said, that he personally attended his friend's autopsy. Why not? Rimann had given the sheriff thirty-eight hundred dollars to help fund the mounted patrol.

As the weeks dragged on, Purdome and his deputies, as well as the city police and the FBI, said they saw signs of an emerging strong-arm war among coin-machine operators in the city. In Jefferson City, officials disclosed that Rimann was not new to the liquor business after all, that he actually had part ownership in 120 taverns in Kansas City.

Word surfaced that he often carried a gun, not far from the money belt strapped around his waist that held large amounts of cash. More talk around town said he knew his life was in jeopardy. His wife said that she and her husband had been followed in the past in their car, and that while her husband was unnerved, he was beginning to pick up on threats.

At the state capital, Missouri governor Forrest Smith demanded that "necessary changes" be made in Kansas City law enforcement to make an arrest in the Rimann murder. He even sent state troopers to Kansas City to help out. "Call upon the sheriff of Jackson County or any other county in this state, the prosecuting attorney and all law enforcement agencies," the governor instructed.

But the case bogged down. "At a Halt in Probe" reported the *Star*. Then came another headline, "Reach Dead End in Probe." Right above that story was an announcement that the Rimann will had been filed and Esther stood poised to inherit most of the jackpot, the remainder to be put into a trust for their son.

Not long afterward came yet another short newspaper revelation. It was the biggest stunner of all. It said, "Wedding bells will ring soon for J. A. Purdome, 52, Jackson County sheriff, and Mrs. Esther L. Rimann, 42, widow of Wolf C. Rimann, juke box operator who was slain in gangland fashion here . . ."

She was recently widowed. He was recently divorced. They were married in a small ceremony in the tearoom of the Hotel Muehlebach. She wore a two-piece light navy-blue suit, fur neckpiece, and an orchid corsage. She wore a black velvet hat. The sheriff was dressed in a suit, and four of his deputies stood by his side at the fireplace during the double-ring ceremony. The couple said they had become friendly way back when Purdome was still a liquor license inspector and her husband, Wolf, was the golf professional at the Hillcrest club. She also liked golf, and the sheriff joked that "I'm going to take up the game seriously next year." For now it was off to Union Station and a ten-day honeymoon in the South.

They returned as man and wife in late 1950, having waited to exchange vows until after the Kefauver committee had come and left Kansas City. That was for appearance's sake, and also because the sheriff and many of his deputies were busy being called as witnesses before the crime committee in the federal courthouse. The deputies were big men, fat men actually, many obese, and they could not be missed waddling into the hearing room, many so large they could barely stuff themselves into a police uniform.

Deputy Jack Brice was a tough, gruff Irishman who was a lead investigator into my grandfather's death. He was teased around the sheriff's station as "Jackie Gleason." He also served as one of the sheriff's groomsmen at his wedding to the Rimann widow. Deputy Clark Johnson owned a liquor store on the side. He also liked to go out to the eastern part of Jackson County, near Lake Tapawingo, and kill time with other gamblers playing "mouse games." Men bet cash on little mice racing on little tracks. But there was nothing small about Deputy Johnson. He weighed 425 pounds. Everybody called him "Tiny."

Mike Randazzo (no weight given) had been a deputy sheriff for six years, appointed by Purdome, and he worked nights at the sheriff's headquarters in the downtown courthouse, "watching over things," he said. He enjoyed the work. Stress-free, he said. Easy as pie, and the deputies knew a lot about pie. So laid-back was Deputy Randazzo, even though he was on vacation when someone blew the vault in the sheriff's office, that when he returned to work he did not even bother to ask about it. Never saw it in the newspaper, either, he said. "I don't remember this instance," Deputy Randazzo said flat out.

Kefauver's chief investigator, George H. White, jumped in. "Just a minute, Mr. Randazzo," White said. "This is straining our credulity a little too far to think that the deputy sheriff who has been ordinarily for six years on duty at night in a courthouse where the ballots were stolen, where the sheriff's safe was blown, would not even discuss the matter with his fellow deputies after his return to work."

Randazzo did not budge. He held his ground. "I was not interested in anything like that," he said.

White pressed him further. He suggested that if the committee found any links between Randazzo and the blown safe, it would not be pretty. "Then you would be in some trouble," White warned him.

"I realize that," said Randazzo, unfazed.

"You don't want to be in any trouble, do you?"

"I do not. Never was in any trouble in my life."

But the implied threat apparently softened Randazzo; it got him to concede there was talk about ineptness in Purdome's sheriff's department. "I just heard about the safe being blown in the courthouse," Randazzo admitted now. "And there was some sarcastic comments, you know, that the sheriff's office up on the top floor didn't hear the explosion. Stuff like that."

Randazzo also conceded that he liked to hang around the local political clubs and that he had known the two Charlies—Binaggio and Gargotta. But he said he steered clear of the underworld. "I play a little cards once in a while," he said. But "I don't gamble," and "I just play at home." He insisted, "I don't do much of anything but stay at home, go to shows or prize fights."

He said Purdome gave him his deputy's badge for his work in local Democratic politics. "That is how I am holding my job," he boasted to the crowded committee hearing, "by being a precinct captain."

Chairman Kefauver, who in six years would be the Democratic nominee for vice president, joined in at this point. "We are not going to put up with any monkey business," he lectured the witness.

Still, Randazzo, the right politician for the right deputy sheriff's job, held his ground. "If I knew anything I would really tell the truth," he promised the chairman. "If I discussed the ballot boxes with anybody, the ballots, whatever it is, with anybody, I would be more than glad to tell you. . . . But I don't remember me discussing the ballot boxes because I wasn't interested in them."

Another to testify was Harry W. Hundley, a former Kansas City police official who had changed jobs and went to work for Rimann's jukebox and pinball-machine business. Later in 1959 he was charged with operating a "tourist court" west of Springfield, Missouri, that actually was a house of prostitution. Around the same time he was sent to prison for ten years for sticking up a poker game in West Plains, Missouri.

But before all that Hundley served as a Kansas City policeman for five years and was close to the sheriff's office. In fact, as he told the Kefauver committee, he always considered deputy sheriffs "friends of mine," and said that Rimann had placed "three or four" of the deputies on the Rimann payroll. "They drew monthly pay," Hundley said. They also "rode the county and helped get locations" for the company to place more slot machines and jukeboxes in more bars. "They would call us and tell us to go out and see so and so," he said of the deputies.

Even Sheriff Purdome would make himself available, sometimes two or three times a week. "When I am over at the courthouse I will go upstairs and see him, maybe eat my lunch up there at the jail."

Other times the sheriff came to him, he said, especially after Rimann was killed and the company was being administered by his widow in her new capacity as head of her husband's estate.

"That is Mrs. Rimann?" Kefauver asked.

"Yes, sir."

"She operates it?"

"Yes, sir."

"Do you know what business the sheriff has in coming around to see you two or three times a week?"

"Sheriff Purdome and Mrs. Rimann go together."

"Mr. Rimann and the sheriff were very close friends?"

"That is true."

Hundley added, "I am in and out of the office. I see Purdome, I would say, three, four times a week."

Asked Kefauver, "What does he do there?"

"Oh, he just comes in, usually to pick up Mrs. Rimann."

But it was more than that. The committee alleged that Purdome actually had a ten thousand–dollar interest in Rimann's new liquor wholesaling business. To get to that they finally called the boss himself to the stand. For two long sessions Sheriff Purdome appeared as the committee's last but star witness, and as he testified he fiddled with his fingers, twitched his eyes, and bit his lips. At times he curled his feet under the chair. Some questions he tried to dodge.

"Wolf Rimann, he was a good friend of yours, I presume?" asked Rudolph Halley, the committee's chief counsel.

"Yes, a very good friend," Purdome said.

The sheriff told how he routinely gave out special deputy badges to fifty or seventy-five "prominent businessmen in Kansas City." He said it was a function carried over from past days. "We rather encouraged it during the war, during civilian defense," Purdome said.

Halley asked, "How would it help law enforcement to have Wolf Rimann having a siren and a red light on his automobile?"

"In case we ever needed him to use it in an emergency," Purdome answered, "I could have called on him."

Purdome said he learned only a month before Rimann was killed that some of the sheriff's deputies were on the Rimann payroll, and that they were making up to thirteen hundred dollars in extra take-home cash. "I told them to discontinue the practice," the sheriff said. Then he sought to justify that very practice. "It isn't a violation at all, as I look upon it. But it isn't a very wholesome situation," either.

Purdome answered questions about several local bars, the White House and the Plantation and the Half Hill Tavern, too, places that the committee said Purdome and his deputies had let operate freely with wide-open gambling and other illegal games of chance. Purdome tried to brush them off. He stalled for a bit. "If the committee has a few minutes of time," he said, "I might give you a list of a few places that I have raided and closed."

Purdome also had ready-made excuses for the blown vault and the stolen ballots. "I thought the door was quite secure," he said.

The senators raised their eyebrows.

Well, the sheriff added, "I am not a lock expert."

The committee dug deeper. Kefauver wanted to know just what was going on between him and Mrs. Rimann, his soon-to-be wife, and the jukebox and slot-machine operation. What was his cut?

"I have no interest in the business other than Mrs. Rimann and I are very good friends," he said.

"You go around for the purpose of helping out with the business, or what?" the chairman asked.

"No."

"Advising her about the operation of the business?"

"No. I usually go by there in the evening to pick Mrs. Rimann up."

"You and she are very good friends?'

Here he told the truth. "Oh, yes, yes," he said.

Still they were not done with him. The committee had learned that Purdome was padding his wallet with thousands of dollars in county fees. They asked him, why not give it back to the taxpayers?

"I feel that it is mine," he told the committee. He had no intention of refunding the money. "I am entitled to it," he said.

The sheriff and his deputies, the committee charged, seemed wholly incapable of bringing anyone to justice. From the dais an irritated Senator Charles Tobey leaned into Purdome. "I am telling you, Mr. Sheriff," he said. "Officials like you aren't worth anything for public morale, to let these birds get away with everything, and then you come before us and sit down and cushion yourself upon our table. I get tired of it myself. It smells unto heaven."

Purdome bit his lip and curled his toes. "I possibly have done as much for law enforcement in Kansas City and Missouri as any other man," he protested.

The senator scoffed. "That is not very high, apparently," he said. "From all the criminal records it has been very poor in this county with Binaggio and Gargotta and Tom, Dick and Harry playing their rotten games."

Purdome felt cornered. "Well, of course," he said, "those things might be true. We can't deny those facts . . ."

Tobey hit him on the stolen ballots, and Purdome weakly explained that the vote records were taken from the basement, "and our office is on the 11th floor."

Tobey kept at him. "What did you do about it?" he asked.

"There has been nothing developed," Purdome said.

"How hard did you try?"

"We worked pretty hard on it," the sheriff said.

But he could not offer much in the way of any investigative details. In fact, in a community often terrorized by hoodlums and gangsters, Purdome could not even name any potential suspects.

"Really I don't know anyone," he told the senator. "I can't think of any name right now."

Tobey was not buying it. "So you, the sheriff of this county, in view of what has happened, can't think of anyone you think might be guilty of this thing?" he asked, his voice rising.

Tobey told Purdome point-blank what he thought of him: "Your mental ability is suspect."

And the sheriff could not defend himself. He said, "You tell me that I am sheriff, which is true, but I am charged with a pretty big job." He started making little excuses. "I have 26 men to engage in law enforcement work. There is patrol work, handling traffic and everything else, and answering fight calls and everything else."

Tobey promised him that if Purdome could not come up with some answers, and soon, then the committee would hear from him again. "I'm telling you, Mr. Sheriff, we are going to find out and this committee is going to find out, and some people around Kansas City are going to have a hot time of it in the next six months. I hope your health is good for the next six months. We are going to see you again."

Equally unimpressed was the chairman, Senator Kefauver, like Purdome a fellow Democrat. He summed up the hearings by praising the city police department, and top officers like Nesbitt. "Kansas City today, I think, is a clean city," he concluded, "with the people greatly interested in law enforcement and backing up their police department, and you have a good police department in the city."

But he had not one kind word for Purdome and his county law enforcement operation. "I do not think much can be said for the sheriff or for law enforcement in the county," he said. In a mocking aside to Purdome, whom Kefauver clearly had little taste for, the chairman said he had come to these conclusions "with all due reference to the personable sheriff who appeared here."

He spoke for a while about Kansas City's dark past as a boss-controlled city, of the old Pendergast machine and the surge of the Italian Mafia. Kansas City, he said, deserved better.

He said that when sheriff's deputies placed themselves on the mob payroll, scaring tavern owners into doing business with gangsters, the sheriff should be held accountable for cleaning up his own shop. Instead, he said, Purdome stood silent, and by his silence acquiesced to the rotten arrangement and the stench of paybacks hovering around his elected office. These deputies should have been fired, Kefauver said.

He warned the good people of Kansas City that the criminal influence had compromised Purdome's office, and that it "does not reflect credit on the sheriff or on the type of law enforcement you have."

In closing, the committee confronted Purdome with the list of unsolved slayings. What kind of homicide department did his sheriff's office have, anyway? It did not sound like much to them.

Here in reading the transcripts I paused again. I set down the bound galleys. I gazed up at the vaulted marble ceiling of the Library of Congress. Had I been in that hearing that day, sitting in front of Jackson County sheriff J. A. Purdome, thinking about how he and his deputies had supposedly "investigated" my grandfather's death, I would have made this the million-dollar question. That is exactly what I would have asked him: What kind of homicide bureau are you running?

Purdome did not give the kind of answer I would have wanted. He just shrugged. To him, the unsolved deaths piling up in Kansas City and in the county did not seem to be such a big deal. "In our rather feeble way we continue to work on them," he said.

Feeble, indeed.

The committee in its official report had more to say, determining that Purdome and his deputies had "prostituted their oaths of office when they were supposed to serve the public."

Blown vaults and stolen ballots, unsolved homicides, a mob hit in the middle of the afternoon, a new bride.

And a prisoner out cold in the jailhouse basement.

And still Kefauver would not ease up on Sheriff Purdome. The senator was emerging as a national political figure, and he wrote a book about his racketeering hearings. He called it *Crime in America,* and he devoted chapter 10 to "Kansas City, the law of the jungle."

Kansas City, he said, "had fallen under the influence of as vicious a bunch of criminals as existed anywhere. The Kansas City mob, led by men who were high up in the Mafia, milked the town." Kefauver called Rimann "a local racketeer and juke-box and pinball king." He said Purdome "was notably lax in his enforcement of the liquor and gambling laws." And how cozy and how romantic that love had blossomed among the ruins of the sheriff's law enforcement department, and that "Sheriff Purdome married Rimann's widow." Kefauver said elected officials like Purdome, and not shady figures like Rimann, "were supposed to serve the public."

For two years the words from the powerful Senate leader echoed over Jackson County politics, two years to allow a reform candidate to rise up and challenge the entrenched sheriff in 1952. His name was Arvid Owsley. He had absolutely no prior training in law enforcement; the closest he ever came to a badge and a uniform was his stint as an army sergeant during World War II. Arvid Owsley was a lawyer and not a peace officer. He was born in Macon, Missouri, and in 1936 he earned a law degree from the University of Missouri, and a few years after that he moved to Kansas City. Here he toiled quite inconspicuously in the state's attorney general's office. The one and last time he had ever been elected to anything was in 1936, when he won the rather inconsequential seat of city attorney in tiny Chillicothe, Missouri.

But Owsley did not go unnoticed. He weighed 350 pounds and more. He needed a Cadillac or a Lincoln Continental to rumble around town in. At home in Kansas City he filled up a large green leather chair and ottoman that could handle his heavy bulk. He was as big as any of Purdome's deputies—bigger than most, in fact. So large, they called him "Hippo." He was Hippo Owsley and he never complained. He just laughed and reveled in the nickname. "With a pseudonym like Hippo," he liked to joke, "I never thought I would get a better one."

But it was not his girth or his good humor that made him a strong candidate in the Democratic primary for Jackson County sheriff. A group of Democratic operatives unhappy with the old structure had split from the debris of the crumbling Pendergast regime and formed their own Democratic coalition. They chose Hippo to head their new ticket. "Stop Pendergast-Purdome Rule," proclaimed their political flyers and banners and yard signs stuck in front lawns around the city. "Vote Owsley."

It was a raucous contest, but Hippo did not even have to open his great mouth during the summer campaign. He did not roar; indeed, he rarely spoke.

Purdome did all the talking.

In Jackson County politics everything comes down to the August Democratic primary. On July 15, the *Star*, never having forgotten the words of Senator Kefauver and not shy about addressing Purdome's weak performance during the crime hearings, let him have it. "To a metropolitan county nothing is more dangerous than political subversion of law enforcement," the paper editorialized. "As for Purdome, we can't recall a single action to redeem his miserable showing before the Kefauver committee. With specific details the hearing illuminated a situation that had been largely known and partly suspected for years."

The paper complained that over the past two years Purdome had done little to clean up his department. Taverns in the rural areas patrolled by his deputies still stayed open well past midnight and were only loosely regulated. The indicted deputies remained free. "Particularly irritating" was Purdome's personal slice of the money paid to house federal prisoners in the sheriff's county jail.

"A sheriff holds one of the highest positions of public trust in Jackson County—a vital law enforcement office. The evidence of Purdome's past administration raises new fears of how he would use his office in another full term."

A week later the bottom of Purdome's campaign cracked wide open when nine dangerous prisoners cut their way out of his county jail atop the courthouse. They used an acetylene torch to burn bars and slide out, one after the other just around midnight on the twelfth floor of the detention center. Purdome's night jailer, sixty-six-year-old Patrick Ruane, was quickly overcome.

Deputy Ruane told Purdome that one of the prisoners had called out to him in the night. William Stover was being held in the county jail's "Hole." It was known as the Hole only because the cell had no drinking fountain. Stover said he was thirsty and wanted a drink of water, and when jailer Ruane approached him one of the other already freed prisoners, Irson K. Roberts, popped him on the head, choked him with a towel, and grabbed his set of jail corridor keys. They tied his wrists with copper wire, and the escape was on.

"They told me that if I moved they would kill me," Ruane told his boss.

These were not the lovable drunks like my grandfather, unable to pay a small municipal court fine. These were not prisoners who drove too fast or stole hats or did not pay their speeding tickets, like those working in the corn and onion fields out at the Kansas City Municipal Farm. These were real criminals, hardened types awaiting trial on felony charges that included rape and kidnapping and narcotics. One was serving a year of county time for assault. Another was being held after authorities realized he had critical information about four local murders, including the still-unsolved slayings of the two Charlies.

Mike Randazzo, the night deputy working on the floor below the escape, heard nothing unusual upstairs. He did not even learn about the jailbreak until Stover, one of the escapees, called him on Randazzo's desk phone sometime later and told him that nine prisoners had cleared the jail and he'd better get up there and untie

Deputy Ruane. Randazzo, of course, was the same deputy who did not know anything about the blown vault in the courthouse, either.

Most curious of all was how a former inmate, Ivory "Seldom Seen" Johnson, had taught the other inmates how to fashion a jail key from a toothbrush and the teeth of a comb. Johnson had just been convicted of murder and was given a life sentence and knew he was about to be leaving for Jefferson City. Before he caught that prison bus he made a chewing-gum impression of a jail key that one of the deputies had "inadvertently" left lying around. He told them to give the gum impression enough time to harden and then apply it to the comb and brush and make a sturdy key.

Seldom Seen had one last parting wish for his pals. Good luck, he said.

They used the gum and toothbrush key to open their cell doors and then discovered the acetylene torch among welding equipment left in a nearby jail conference room. That allowed them to burn their way out of the steel doors in the hallway and steal down the fire escape. The escapees eventually were rounded up; some made it as far as Texas before they were caught.

And still, the *Star* kept lambasting Purdome. "The sheriff's office is a challenge to the people of Jackson County," the newspaper editorialized. "They don't have to tolerate the kind of perverted and political law enforcement they have known under J. A. Purdome." The sheriff's "over-all record" was their major concern. "In politics some of the sheriff's boys have played a rough game. . . . On its face the evidence points to an untrustworthy sheriff's office. It is the type of record to destroy public confidence in county law enforcement."

The Hippo stood on the sidelines, and he did not speak. He did not have to. As the prisoners were rearrested they began to tell stories about drinking whiskey in the jail; one of them in on a murder charge bragged that he had three fifth bottles and six pints of whiskey stashed back at the jail, awaiting his return.

A shame-faced Purdome had to admit that there were indeed several half pints that had been taken in an earlier sheriff's raid and were being stored in a jail closet. He insisted, though, that the inmates would never have had access to that closet.

The prisoners also said they shared cigarettes and money in the jail, though money was supposed to be strictly forbidden. The cash, the inmates said, was to buy the jail whiskey. And the whiskey, they said, they purchased from the deputies. The deputies charged them eight dollars for a pint, and twice that much for a fifth. What's more, sometimes the deputies drank with them.

Deputy Richard J. O'Brien admitted as much, and told investigators that he had been imbibing the night of the escape. "I had a couple drinks of whiskey at home before going to work . . . and took a half-pint bottle of whiskey about half full," he said. He added that a fellow deputy, Herman J. "Wimpy" Wayland, confronted him the night of the jailbreak. Wayland asked O'Brien if he was under the influence.

"Why sure," O'Brien told him.

O'Brien said there was no reason to lie because Wayland "could smell it on me" and that "I told Wimpy I had brought a couple of shots with me and I had them in a bottle in my pocket."

Asked about the drinking and carousing in his jail, Purdome claimed the booze came from twenty-five cases taken in a raid last Christmas. He admitted that more was still being stored in the jail, including a fifth of Four Roses, some of the best Kentucky straight bourbon ever distilled. "If there was any whiskey drinking it had to be stolen from that locker," Purdome said.

The Hippo smiled on the side but still did not open his great mouth, not even when agents from the Federal Bureau of Investigation entered the case because of the jailhouse drinking and deputies selling drinks to inmates. By now three prisoners and at least one deputy had owned up to the booze and liquor sales.

Purdome fired two deputies for drinking, and fraternizing with prisoners and the Hippo still did not say a word. But others did. The *Warrensburg (Mo.) Daily Star-Journal* said that "Purdome's efforts toward really effective law enforcement have been as faint as a young lamb's bleat."

In Chicago, James M. Pendergast, heir to the old regime that was backing Purdome, hinted that the organization might throw in the towel on the sheriff. Pendergast was attending the Democratic National Convention that was nominating Harry Truman for president, and he said on the floor of the convention that he and a group of close advisers were considering telephoning Purdome and suggesting that he drop out.

Next to be heard was the Kansas City Crime Commission, an organization made up of area law enforcement officials. The commission on July 26 issued a report saying Purdome's "enforcement of the laws in Jackson County has been extremely inefficient." In fact, they complained, Purdome was the only local high-ranking law enforcement officer who did not cooperate with the commission in fighting crime.

The commission cited the jailbreak but also mentioned the Kefauver findings and how liquor dealers and the gambling joints continued to operate freely with little or no regulation. The commission dug further and revealed that twenty-one of Purdome's deputies had been hired even though they had accumulated prior arrest records "other than for traffic offenses." Eight of his honorary deputies had past arrests for serious crimes, the panel said. And one of his "special deputies is a reputed leader of the Mafia organization in Kansas City." They noted that Purdome was "far more concerned" with promoting a new stadium in Riverside, Missouri, where he held a large financial stake, and his continued involvement in his new wife's work running Rimann's old jukebox and slot-machine enterprise. "Without reservation we do not feel that J. A. Purdome is a qualified candidate for the office of sheriff of Jackson County," concluded crime commission chairman E. M. Dodds.

Purdome refused to withdraw. He would not be hounded out. On the eve of the August 5 primary he went on television—a novelty in 1952—and spoke for fifteen minutes about why he should be rewarded with a third term. He blasted the *Star* as a Republican newspaper and said that although the jail escape looked bad, the prisoners were back under wraps. "Every phase is being investigated," Purdome told his television audience. "And if there be guilt on anyone's part, he shall be prosecuted. We expect criticism where such is justified but we will not tolerate persecution."

In large newspaper ads he praised himself as "an honest, efficient and dependable public official." He touted his experience in jail management and his training in business administration. He said his was the "best interest of the public and continued good law enforcement."

And he lost. He was beaten. He was walloped. The final count came in at 54,956 for Owsley and only 33,807 for Purdome. Other votes were spread out among other minor candidates. It was the worst drubbing of all of the Pendergast candidates that season. Even in his own home precinct, the fifth of the Eighth Ward, Purdome took only 46 votes to Owsley's 58. The *Star* called it a "smashing defeat."

So Purdome slunk away. In time he tried to remake himself. By 1960 he returned as an organizer in local Democratic politics. He started to pull his way up one more time, from precinct captain to ward leader and once again into the higher councils of the political party. Then in September 1961, just months into his new post as treasurer of the Jackson County Democratic Committee, he suffered a heart attack. He was sixty-three years old, and he died two weeks later. For the disgraced sheriff, there would be no second act.

His son, Frank Purdome, works as a volunteer at a nursing home in suburban Olathe, Kansas. I had gone to visit my aunt Dorothy Norman and unexpectedly met Frank there helping the residents prepare for Sunday mass. He seemed a good and decent man, and he acknowledged that his father long ago was hooked into the old Pendergast gang. He told me his father loved being sheriff but never talked about it, never discussed unsolved criminal cases or political strategy around the dinner table. Nor did he ever mention the curious death of a prisoner out at the city Farm. "If you bring it home with you, you never leave the job," his father always told Frank. That was the old man's creed. Do not talk about it.

But Jennie Johnson, the widow of the Purdome deputy named Clark Johnson whom everyone called "Tiny," had strong memories, and she did talk. She talked a great deal. She described in an oral history for the Harry S. Truman Library in Independence how her husband would return home and regale her with stories about the sheriff and his crew. "Now, see," she said, "J. A. Purdome was one of the sheriffs that had a lot of these taverns and things. He didn't own them, but I mean . . . he played favorites with them. Yes, very much. Some of these deputies, oh, they were crooked it wasn't even funny. They'd go in and these taverns had to pay off. . . . Oh yes. Lots of them did. A lot of these deputy sheriffs did. They made a lot of money . . ."

Hundley, the former Kansas City police official who later worked for Rimann, had memories, too. One of the last things he told the Kefauver Committee was about the time he attended a large state-wide law enforcement conference in Jefferson City. Purdome was sheriff, and he sent a detective named Delahunty to the state capital to participate. "I heard Delahunty get up and say that he was the superintendent of the homicide division of the Jackson County Sheriff's office," Hundley recalled with a big grin. "Well, up to that time none of us, the police officers, knew there was a homicide unit. We all laughed!"

Crooked, fat, and inept. This was the sheriff and these were the deputies who were going to solve my grandfather's death?

CHAPTER 7

On Wednesday, May 26, 1948, there appeared in the morning paper a small four-paragraph item that ran deep in the inside pages. Headlined "Dies at Municipal Farm," the *Kansas City Times* reported that James Patrick Lyons, thirty-nine, of Fifth and Main streets, had been arrested the previous Thursday near his home on skid row and that he had been sentenced on Friday to the Farm after being fined fifteen dollars for intoxication. On Monday he was placed in solitary confinement because "he caused a disturbance," the item said. He had been checked by guards six times before he was found dead an hour before sunrise on Tuesday.

The article added that William Delahunty, superintendent of the homicide bureau for the Jackson County sheriff's office, a heavyset man like many of the rest of the deputies, was in charge of the investigation. Like his boss, Sheriff Purdome, Delahunty was deeply active in Jackson County Democratic politics. He had run the Fifth Ward for the party. He served as secretary-treasurer of the First Ward Business Men's Democratic Club. With that kind of political background, and this an election year and his boss up before the voters again, Delahunty wasted no time announcing what he said had happened to my grandfather.

Delahunty was born and raised in the Kansas City area. He knew its ins and outs, its street corners and its neighborhoods, and he knew its skeletons, too. He knew how to hide things. Also like Purdome, Delahunty had worked his way up in law enforcement. When he first started out in public service he was assigned to the Kansas City Health Department, an agency with a good deal of oversight of the Municipal Farm. Delahunty knew how things worked out there as well.

In 1933 he was named chief inspector for the city Health Department. Six years later he moved over to the sheriff's office just as

Purdome's star was rising. There Delahunty stayed for twenty years and served as a deputy and then as chief deputy of the criminal division and now as superintendent of the homicide bureau.

His career closely tracked Purdome's. In many ways the men were inseparable. They were so tight that Purdome gave Delahunty the honor of serving as one of his groomsmen at the hotel tearoom when the sheriff married Wolf Rimann's widow.

So it was to Purdome's advantage and it fell to Delahunty's doing that the homicide investigation into my grandfather's death be quietly swept aside. They clearly wanted to dispose of the whole unexplainable, messy affair. Here it already was late May, just a little more than two months out from the crucial August Democratic primary. Voters would be going to the polls soon.

In that very first small newspaper item about the jailhouse death, Delahunty tried to quickly close the lid on the case. "Natural causes," he announced.

The death certificate offered the barest of facts. But death by natural causes was not among them. It described James Lyons as divorced, yet a spouse, identified only as Josephine, was listed on the form. For the box asking whether she was still alive, the coroner's office typed in a question mark. His "usual occupation" was listed as "railroad work," and they said his parents were from Ireland. His birthday was June 18, 1908 (mine is June 17), he was not a veteran, and his Social Security number, if he had one, was "unknown."

More important, the coroner determined the "immediate cause of death as shock . . . fractured neck . . . presumably of unknown traumatic conditions."

Means of injury: "Trauma."

Time of death: 5:30 in the morning, May 25, 1948.

He had lived thirty-nine years, eleven months, and six days.

His body would be turned over to his mother.

There was no mention of solitary confinement in the death certificate, no description of a struggle. No evidence of a rope, a noose, or a chair tipped over. Under the category of accident, suicide, or homicide, Jackson County coroner James C. Walker wrote simply: "Do not know."

Armed with the death certificate, I drove out to the cemetery office in Kansas City, Kansas, and found an old printed graveyard register that said my grandfather had died of a "broken neck."

I visited the funeral home and their records called it a "fractured neck." Their file added this notation: "On insurance papers, fractured neck presumably unknown traumatic conditions at Municipal Farm."

I went back to the public libraries and started feeding old microfilm rolls into the readers, scanning the *Star* and its morning edition, the *Kansas City Times*, for more stories from the week that he died. That is how I came upon Delahunty's instant and untested declaration that foul play was out of the question. The man died naturally, Delahunty said.

The next day a smaller item, this one just three paragraphs, was printed in the papers. "Lyons died Tuesday in a cell at the Municipal Farm," it said. "An autopsy indicated he had suffered a broken neck."

Yet there was no announcement of a police investigation. Instead, the stories ended that week, followed by a few obituary notices. The rosary was said at 8 P.M. at the funeral home. The funeral Mass was held at 7:45 the next morning at venerable old St. Thomas. He was buried out at Mt. Calvary, alone in a section away from the family plot. They had no room for him.

My newly found cousin, Rick Neumann, gave me the Catholic Burial Service booklet for my grandfather's funeral, inscribed "In Memory of James Patrick Lyons, age 39 years." "Pray for the dead, that they may be loosed from sins," the little missal said, quoting from the book of Machabees in the Old Testament. It also offered prayers "for the poor captive souls in purgatory."

And that was about all I could find in the newspapers that first week, and nothing more. But I could not fathom why the sheriff's homicide squad would not press harder and immediately suspect someone had to have killed the prisoner. I thought to myself: Why not open a murder investigation? Why not question witnesses? Why not polygraph the guards? I mean, how does he break his neck when he is all alone and the jail staff said it kept looking in on his well-being every several hours or so and he seemed fine?

How do you bury a man without an explanation? Why do you shut down a death investigation without asking questions?

People do not just die.

I knew now about my grandfather's fractured neck and the body wounds, but I could not answer the central question—how? Maybe it was some kind of accident, maybe he slipped on a wet floor. But that did not fly. It did not seem plausible.

Maybe he died after a fight then. Common sense told me any jail-house inmate would have protested and struggled mightily to keep from being thrown into solitary confinement. His Irish dander up, my grandfather might have wrestled with the best of the guards. He could have tussled with them during the march down the basement stairs. He likely was handcuffed, and they could have pushed him down the stairwell. They could have tripped him. Maybe at the door to the Hole they shoved him inside and cracked his neck. Maybe that is how they killed him. Or maybe they came in later and silenced him.

But how do I find out?

Several weeks rolled by, and still I could think of nothing. On my long morning walks I tossed it around in my mind, thinking it over and over. What am I missing here? Where do I go next? Who can I call? None of the old records existed out at the Farm. The caves had none of the sheriff's homicide reports, if there ever were any. The county coroner's office files were long gone. Each morning I returned from my walk with empty answers.

I was about to give up.

Then one afternoon I looked once again at my grandfather's death certificate. I stared closer this time at the document and turned it over, and there on the back page my eyes stopped on the signature of a man I recognized from my own past—Blaine E. Weilert. He was a licensed embalmer, and he was the mortician who prepared my grandfather for burial.

When I was a teenager the Weilerts lived across the street from us, and I can still see him yet, the old man pulling into his driveway in the long black sedan, stepping out in the dark suit, a cloud of gray cigar smoke trailing him into the house. I called his son, John, whom I had not seen or spoken to in years, and he agreed to hunt for any records his since-deceased father might have kept. It was a long shot, sure.

But on a Sunday John Weilert called back.

Rick, he said. You need to see something.

John lives on the southeastern rim of the city, past the Ozark Road hilltop and the leveled Municipal Farm prison grounds. His home sits on a steep hill, too, a wooded tract where his large dogs barked at my car pulling up the drive. John is in the burying business him-self, a trustee at Elmwood Cemetery, one of the city's oldest grave-yards. He reined in the dogs and invited me inside.

On the living room mantle rested a portrait of his father. I told John I remembered the cigars.

"Dad constantly smoked," John Weilert said. "As a young man going out to retrieve bodies, he found that the best way to cut the smell of a decaying corpse was the aroma of a good cigar."

John added, "Mom put up with it."

In his day Blaine Weilert ran two funeral homes. One was located on the city's impoverished West Side, not far from the river bottoms. The other was located farther south at Sixty-ninth Street and Troost Avenue, across from a sprawling cemetery not far from our home, the cemetery where now old boss Tom Pendergast lays quiet and still.

To keep business thriving, John said, his father had to remain po-litically active. A loyal Democrat, Blaine Weilert served as president of the First District Veterans Club. A veteran himself, he sometimes spoke at political rallies around town urging everyone to "get out and get every veteran working" when it came election time. Often he opened up his funeral parlor on the predominantly Hispanic West Side of the city for organizational meetings.

Once Weilert started up an American Legion post in honor of a young World War II soldier named Ralph V. Sifuentes. He was killed when his troop ship took enemy fire. Sifuentes was twenty-two years old and married, and he and his wife, Catherine, had a nine-month-old baby. The boy, Ralph Eugene Sifuentes, was born after his father had shipped off. He never saw his father; his father never saw his son. And the family realized something far worse had happened when a Christmas cake they had mailed him overseas was returned unopened.

Blaine Weilert knew community service, and he knew local poli-tics. Whenever a new county coroner was elected, Weilert, like all of his rivals, the other morticians and embalmers and funeral direc-tors, jockeyed for a favored position on the new coroner's good side. That usually meant a bottle of scotch at Christmas or something extra around Election Day. When the poor and the indigent died, or someone was killed mysteriously, it often was the coroner who de-cided which funeral home the body was sent to. The coroner could be a powerful man in these circles. He decided which funeral parlor got the most business. That was how the system worked. That was how they made a living in the dying business.

"Dad," said John, "swam with those fishes."

He also, God love him, buried the poor. Bless him more, he kept meticulous records.

Sitting there at his kitchen table John placed before me a large, legal-size, hardbound maroon funeral registry. It was his father's daily ledger in which he accounted for every embalmment, funeral, and burial he handled. This volume covered nearly four years, 1945 through the first half of 1948.

The book was old and stiff. It creaked when I opened the cover.

Here was a chronicle of the last moments of the city's misbegotten, its poor and its tragic, its lost and its least. Here Blaine Weilert had documented the life and death of many of the city's faithful, people like my grandfather long unremembered. Old Mr. Weilert, the man I watched return home each night in his crisp suit and his funereal air, was, unbeknownst to us, the town historian.

Several times a week he clipped out newspaper obituaries and stories of accidental deaths and pasted them into his books next to the paid classified notices and the free obituaries announcing wakes and masses and graveside services. Some of the clippings were lengthy newspaper articles, while others were just a paragraph or two. Some merited barely a sentence. Alongside the clippings he often attached copies of his bills and receipts and certificates of service. In his books he collected the history that Kansas City forgot.

Slowly, I turned the brittle pages to 1948, the post–World War II years, the time my grandfather would have joined the others in Weilert's big ledger. The city was prospering once more, the Depression over, the war won. The economy was up, and soldiers had returned home from Europe and the South Pacific. There were new jobs to be had and new homes to build; the G.I. bill was putting veterans through college. For people of ambition and newly acquired means, the comfortable 1950s were just around the corner.

But not for those in Weilert's book. From his pages tumbled the grief of lives cut short, or lives lived too long. Their stories rose up from the crowd and the din and the excitement of Kansas City's booming downtown commercial streets, and its poor neighborhoods beyond the city's core. Like my grandfather, they seemed lost in a city rapidly changing, one they could not compete in, yet each tiny voice spoke to me in his own small, unique way.

Some of their deaths could not be explained.

Adalaska Dotson was eighty-three, yet still he worked. He was a music teacher, and he lived in the city's old Quality Hill neighborhood at Fifteenth and Broadway, up on the river bluffs overlooking the rail yards and the meatpacking sprawl. He had belonged to the West Side Christian Church, and he was a member of the Odd Fellows lodge. The only family anyone could find was a sister named Ida Mae Smith. She lived somewhere in Pennsylvania.

Dotson was walking west on Twelfth Street one November evening. He looked spiffy in his tan felt hat and the sheet music tucked smartly under his arm. Around seven o'clock, something or someone came up from behind him, and he was shortly found lying on the sidewalk. His sheet music was scattered about his body. The tan felt hat lay nearby, a hole in the crown where something had struck Dotson sharply in the head.

A neighbor told police that when he found Dotson the old man just seemed dazed. Other witnesses thought maybe he had been grazed by a passing automobile. An ambulance arrived, and they noticed his head was bleeding and his legs and hands discolored. No weapons were found, so police theorized maybe the culprit was a hit-and-run driver. Dotson was taken to the city's General Hospital, and there he died.

A much younger man, thirty-eight-year-old John Harlow, locked himself in his room at the Bray Hotel on the rim of Quality Hill, at Eleventh Street and Baltimore Avenue. A hotel bellboy had been trying to reach him for some time, but Harlow did not answer the telephone or respond to repeated knocks at his door. Finally, the boy let himself in and discovered Harlow slumped in the bathtub. Four empty whiskey bottles were left undisturbed in a dresser drawer.

Why he had come to Kansas City was anyone's guess. Surprisingly, he had been a physician and had worked in two small Louisiana communities. But he had been ill and had been treated as a patient in Topeka. Police surmised he might have slipped and struck his head on the tub. Then an autopsy showed that Dr. John Hyland Harlow, a year younger than my grandfather, had not died accidentally at all. The cause of death was tuberculosis, the same fate that met my uncle. The underlying cause of death was cirrhosis of the liver, a pronouncement sure to meet my grandfather had he lived long enough.

Eighty-five-year-old James "Scotty" Shaw sold newspapers on the streets downtown. Each morning and afternoon he regaled his customers with tales of his adventures as a circus trapeze artist. Born in Scotland, he would laugh and tell how at fourteen he ran off with the Big Top. He met his wife, Harriet, a circus bareback rider who also finessed the tightrope. But over the years he grew too old to fly the trapeze anymore. So for a while he worked as a railroad hand and then, unable to afford retirement, sold papers to get by. Harriet had died years ago.

On May 12, 1948, just a week before my grandfather was arrested and sent to the Farm, Shaw collapsed on the street from a sudden stroke, right in front of his newspaper stand at Eleventh and Baltimore. The *Star* gave him a four-paragraph write-up. They even ran a natty picture of Scotty from his thrilling days in the circus, styled up in a black tuxedo and thin dark tie. He sported a thick, proud mustache, and his eyes were alight with excitement. For thirty years he had lived quietly in Kansas City, the circus long faded away. The only person left to claim him was a daughter in Canada.

There was another Shaw, too, this one just a year old. James E. Shaw Jr., son of Mr. and Mrs. James E. Shaw Sr., died at a quarter to four in the morning. He had somehow wrapped his tiny hands around a bottle of fly spray at the family home at Eighteenth and Baltimore. At the hospital they gave him penicillin for the poison and placed him under an oxygen tent. He died overnight. His father worked as a steel plant mechanic, and the family had little money. Weilert charged just $126.25 to bury the boy in Oak Grove Cemetery. The Shaws were Protestant but had no preacher. They returned the boy to earth's dust with hardly a prayer over him.

So the stories rolled off the pages. A husband killed his ex-wife, a waitress at a Main Street grill, and saved a final bullet for himself. A packinghouse worker accidentally inhaled fumes from liquid ammonia. He collapsed in the bacon-curing cellar, and his panicked coworkers stampeded out of the room.

Jose Delgado moved to Kansas City from Mexico. He lived at the Fox Hotel with my grandfather. At times he worked as a railroad laborer, and he knew the train schedules. Mostly, he was despondent over missing his family in Mexico. In March he was taken with stomach complaints to General Hospital. There he jumped from the fifth floor, and although he broke his back he still survived. The doctors fitted him into a body cast.

But Delgado was determined to jump again. Five weeks later, on May 10, he decided to leap from the sixty-foot Twenty-third Street railroad viaduct. He knew when the trains would be coming, and he timed his fall to make sure one of them hit him. Peering down at the rail yard below, he waited for a passing locomotive, and then he fell through the air. The fall killed him. But he was cheated at the last. The brakeman stopped the train just feet from where Delgado hit the ground. He died still wearing the old body cast.

Saddest of all was what happened to Kathleen Ruth Hobbs. She was a child who lived with her desolate, out-of-work parents in a small wood-and-canvas tent near the Blue River, far south of town at Troost Avenue and 119th Street. Late on the afternoon of April 20, 1948, the toddler wandered off.

Her parents, Mr. and Mrs. Lester Hobbs, had a second child, too, Melvin, and he was nineteen months old. Their father had been unemployed for quite some time, so the family pitched their shack on the banks of the river. Really it was just a squat, bare room, from the newspaper photograph not much larger than a solitary jail cell. It had a clapboard door that pulled open and a wash bucket out front. A cookstove stood off to the side.

Kathleen was three months short of her third birthday. Around five o'clock she was seen playing in a truck parked nearby, and then seen no more. The family called the police, and the police called in bloodhounds and fire department boats and Red Cross volunteers. A sheriff's plane scouted overhead. Boy Scouts joined the all-night search. One of the dogs, named Red Chief, marked a spot on the riverbank, and two rescuers dropped a grappling hook from their boat. They brought up Kathleen's body from under nine feet of muddy water.

But it was not until I turned to the back to the book that I learned why John Weilert the undertaker's son had summoned me to his home this morning. There on one of the last pages his father had attached the largest newspaper clipping of all, from a now defunct, scrappy downtown newspaper called the *Kansas City News-Press*. The article was long, and its headline inked in big block letters, all of it taped down into the ledger book. The tape was fragile and cracked, and it was coming loose around the edges. The page itself was frayed and slightly torn.

But it was readable.

And I read it.

In big bold black capital letters it shouted:

CHECK PRISONER'S DEATH AT THE MUNICIPAL FARM!
CORONER HANDS FINDINGS TO COUNTY PROSECUTOR FOR ACTION!
RAP CITY WELFARE DEPARTMENT

The story quoted a friend of the deceased from the local chapter of Alcoholics Anonymous. "Jimmie Lyons," the man said, "was beaten to death."

CHAPTER 8

Once the guard's flashlight spotted my grandfather's body in solitary confinement, the word quickly began to make the rounds. It spread fast, real fast. It circled first among the guards and then up around the jailhouse cell blocks above the basement Dungeon and then swiftly out onto the streets of the city, too. The news landed hard on skid row.

The next afternoon another man was arrested at Fifth and Main streets. Eugene Boston was handcuffed and taken to the eighth floor on top of the city police headquarters downtown. Police were booking him for public drunkenness, another transient from skid row, they presumed, and just like they had my grandfather only a week earlier, they told him he more than likely was bound for the Kansas City Municipal Farm as well. Eugene Boston was twenty-three years old. He instantly knew what that meant.

Completing all the paperwork was taking time, and Boston was growing anxious. Around eight o'clock he asked to use a telephone. According to police sergeant Harlie Atchison, they escorted Boston to an office so he could phone his family. Boston dialed, but the line was busy.

Sergeant Atchison sat nearby, fingerprinting a female prisoner. His eyes were on the prints and not on Boston, who slid up out of his chair and scooted quietly down the hallway. He walked to a window and pushed open a chain attachment. Because he was young and small enough yet, he managed to squeeze through its six-inch opening. Then he jumped.

A second policeman at the booking desk heard the thud. He ran to the window, looked down into the darkening night, and spotted Boston far below, splayed across a railing on the north side of the building. His right arm was severed, torn straight off. Both his legs were broken. Police took him to General Hospital, and doctors began working on his severe internal injuries as well.

Ninety minutes after the suicide attempt, police called Boston's family. This time the line was not busy. They reached first his mother-in-law, Mrs. Frank Bardwell, and her son, Frank Bardwell Jr. They rushed to the hospital. His wife stayed home. Just ten days earlier, on May 17, she had given birth to their second child, a girl.

Mrs. Bardwell told reporters that Boston had been out of work for several weeks. That morning around half past seven, she said, he had left home trying to obtain employment but found a bottle instead. His last job of work was on a railroad section gang.

But he also was keenly aware of the ways of the police and the routine inside a jail, and he knew what could happen after an arrest. He knew about the Kansas City Municipal Farm. More than likely he had heard what had just happened to a prisoner in solitary confinement out there. He knew these things because during the war Eugene Boston had served as a military policeman. He was discharged in January 1946, and his war service, Mrs. Bardwell said, "had left him nervous." He did not like the police, and he did not like jails anymore.

But how he had gotten himself drunk, she could not say. "He had no money to buy liquor."

Another vagrant, Ray Irvan Zellers, fifty-six years old, was taken around that time to city court after he and five other men were picked up for loitering and sleeping in the lobby of the downtown bus depot on McGee Street. According to police, none of the men had any money or a job or a place to live.

Standing before municipal judge Edmund B. Smith, Zellers said he had been working in Morris, Kansas, for a commissary company on a construction project. He also had worked as a welder in the past, and he originally hailed from Joplin, Missouri. He said that shortly after arriving in Kansas City he spent what little cash he had and slept nights at the bus station.

Judge Smith fined Zellers a dollar and ordered him held at the Farm for one day; then he would be released for having served out his fine. As Farm prisoners go, he was getting off lucky, or so it seemed.

Officers moved him briefly into a holding cell with fifteen other prisoners on the fifth floor of police headquarters, and moments later they heard the sound of a falling body. Thud! Zellers had dropped unconscious to the floor, surrounded by the other inmates. An ambulance rushed him to General Hospital, but it was too late for Ray Irvan Zellers, too. The coroner's office was called, and Zellers was pronounced dead. He died of a massive cerebral hemorrhage. No prison Farm for him.

News of my grandfather's death was also rattling the prison population inside the Farm. Tensions there were aboil, and just three days after they carried James Lyons out of the Hole, two inmates made a break for it.

George O. Treece, thirty-five years old, and Willard Mansfield, thirty-three, were supposed to be doing thirty days each for public intoxication when they raced off. They were caught at Fifteenth Street and Prospect Avenue, resentenced to sixty days apiece on the escape charges and, unhappily no doubt, sent back to the Farm. A week later, the inmates appealed their longer sentences, and the case was assigned to Jackson County circuit judge Ben Terte.

Terte was a no-nonsense kind of man. He started his legal career in a downtown law firm and the law was his life, and it seemed he remained a bachelor for the longest time, well into his forties. That was when he happened to meet his future bride, Irene, on a summer cruise ship aboard the steamer *Rotterdam*. They were sailing for Russia. She was an artist and an actress, and as Mrs. Ben Terte she enjoyed "going to the courtroom and watch my husband conduct court."

The son of a Kansas City merchant, Terte loved sneaking off down to the courthouse when he was a boy and marveling at the attorneys arguing their cases. He was graduated from the old University of Kansas City law school in 1914 and was elected a Jackson County judge a dozen years later. Terte was backed by Boss Pendergast even though he never sought his support. He sat on the bench for thirty-five years.

There he ran a tight ship, and lawyers knew to be careful whenever the judge started to lose his cool. He had this way of signaling his impatience. Judge Terte would push his eyeglasses high on top of his forehead and begin to stare at a witness. There was little he missed, and a lot that he absorbed.

On this day the first Municipal Farm escapee, George Treece, testified in front of Judge Terte that he had simply been homesick. He did not mean to escape, he said, not really. But he did walk off to visit his family.

In front of the judge the prisoner rolled up his right pants leg and showed the courtroom a half-healed wound and scar midway to his thigh. That, he told the judge, came from leg irons that the guards put him in after he was caught and returned to the Farm.

Judge Terte looked astounded. "You mean just for walking away from the Farm they treat you like that?" he asked.

The judge turned to assistant city counselor Byron Mintonye and warned, "I don't particularly want to criticize the conduct of Farm policies. But isn't this rather rough treatment for a prisoner sent there on an intoxication charge?"

"Well," the city attorney began, "they escaped . . ."

The judge cut him off. "You mean they walked away," Judge Terte barked. "I have a special aversion to that kind of treatment of human beings. That's a kind of treatment you'd hardly expect outside of Russia or other Communist-dominated countries."

The judge changed the escape charges to absenteeism. He reduced the sixty-day sentences for fleeing to a single extra day of jail time for both men, and then he released the prisoners for time served.

Out at the Farm, where concerns were rising over one man dead in the Hole and now two fresh escapees, Warden Provyn tried to calm things down. He told reporters that prisoners were well aware of the penalties for running, underscoring the fact that "out here they know that solitary confinement and a bread-and-water diet follow escape."

Besides, he said, leg irons fit around the ankle and not the calf, so who knows how Treece cut his leg? Anyway, the warden said, Treece had been sent to the Farm for several arrests on public drunkenness in the past and had run off at least four times. As he recalled, he said, Treece came to the Farm with his leg already in bad shape; no one hurt him here, the warden maintained.

Provyn went on to castigate both prisoners. He said Treece and Mansfield had been trustees and were not subjected to normal Farm restrictions when they bolted this last time. They took advantage of our trust, he said, and tough penalties—leg irons, he meant—were the consequence.

He also released records on the two prisoners. Treece had a string of thirteen previous arrests. He had done time in Oklahoma for burglary and in nearby Leavenworth, Kansas, for violating the federal Mann Act. He had taken a woman across state lines for "immoral purposes." He was not just some town drunk, Provyn said. But Mansfield was. He had been arrested several times for public intoxication.

But the warden had far larger problems on his hands, and he knew it. For the first time in his years as superintendent of the Farm, even as far back as when he was a guard, a prisoner had been carried out on a stretcher in a death neither he nor anyone else could explain.

When sheriff's homicide detectives released my grandfather's body, Jackson County coroner James C. Walker sent it to the Weilert funeral home on the West Side. He met it there, as did Dr. A. E. Upsher, at that time Kansas City's most preeminent pathologist. There in the basement they lifted the corpse onto a porcelain table, its top punctured with holes like a metal screen to drain away the blood and other life fluids. The doctors prepared their instruments. For two hours the doctors would be at work here.

Dr. Walker was the elected county coroner, but he was not a pathologist. That was not required; all anyone needed back then to be a Missouri state coroner was enough votes every four years come November.

Dr. Walker did practice medicine—for nearly sixty years. He lived to be ninety. He was born in Platte County, Missouri, and had been graduated from Tulane University and served as a navy lieutenant during World War I. But mostly he lived all of his life in the Kansas City area.

A political novice, he ran in 1944 as a Democrat and with the blessing and financial support from the Pendergast organization. Dr. Walker easily won the coroner's job.

Now four years had passed, and Dr. Walker was assisting at Weilert's funeral home. He was watching as Dr. Upsher began the autopsy. Dr. Walker also was thinking. The coroner was mindful he was running for reelection. And just like Sheriff Purdome, Dr. Walker had his own political troubles. But unlike the sheriff, Walker had dared to buck the political bosses. And that prompted old Pendergast loyalists to begin withdrawing their political backing of Dr. Walker. They were disappointed because he kept refusing to release bodies that he had investigated in questionable deaths to an undertaker favored by the political machine. That undertaker was Joe Tigerman, and he was an ally of Tim Moran, a longtime Pendergast lieutenant.

Moran had been extremely close to Boss Tom. The two men had grown up together during the battles of the old ward politics. He was one of Pendergast's first and most loyal henchmen. In return the boss squeezed him into lucrative jobs as the city's chief garbage inspector and as building director at the county courthouse downtown. In his spare time Moran also ran a tavern and gambling hall on Prospect Avenue where many of the Pendergast principals would meet to hoist a beer, roll the dice, and spin tales of political intrigue.

In his old age Moran had mentored a young political buck named Joe Tigerman, and when Moran announced that he was retiring from politics and getting out of it altogether, the political favors were supposed to be funneled to Tigerman. Tigerman was an undertaker and he was moving up in the Pendergast ranks, and that meant that Dr. Walker the coroner was expected to send Tigerman plenty of the bodies. To borrow John Weilert's description, that is how the fishes swam.

Tigerman felt he was owed the Pendergast spoils. The more bodies that Dr. Walker would send him, the more money he would make. The more money he made, the more he could line his funeral coat. And more money could be kicked back to the old Pendergast crowd.

Tigerman was a scrawny, thin, balding fellow. He loved politics, especially the Labor Day picnics the Democrats threw each year out at the city's expansive Swope Park. Everyone was invited, and Tigerman loved them so much he described them to a reporter with all the gusto of a small-town booster. He sounded almost like a used-car dealer, which is exactly what he also did on the side. "Listen. Just listen," Tigerman said of the picnics. "Twenty thousand hot dogs! Got that? Then 300 gallons of beer and 550 loaves of bread! Right? But get this. They drank 4,800 bottles of cola, and $550 worth of beer. But here's the clincher—1,136 watermelons! Think of that a minute—1,136 watermelons. They ate everything."

Joe Tigerman loved to make money, lots of money. "It takes a lot of money for me to get along," he was heard to boast.

He also had his troubles with the law. He shipped stolen cars across state lines and drew a three-year federal probation. A federal grand jury identified him as a local bookmaker and said he solicited wagers from his funeral parlor on Prospect. In 1947, the year before this summer's Democratic primary, Tigerman was indicted with a hundred others for vote fraud. He needed money all the more. "I've got troubles," he moaned. "Everybody thinks everybody else is a big man."

Fifteen years down the road the owner of the Tigerman funeral home, who always came to his parlor dressed in white shirt and black tie, was killed. He was shot at close range in the stomach, the bullet hole clean through his necktie and white shirt. He was slain in the inner office of his car dealership. But his assailants did not leave until the job was finished. To make sure Joe Tigerman was dead, they hit him with two more blasts in the head. He died with a ball-point pen in his hand. Near his body in a right-hand desk drawer his automatic pistol remained untouched; Tigerman never had time to grab it. Out front his big red Buick sedan was stolen.

Such was the kind of life Tigerman lived, and Dr. Walker did not want to do business with the man. The coroner did not care to send him all of the bodies just because he had solid political connections. But the coroner would not be bowed, either. He stayed in the race for reelection anyway. He wanted another term, and he was not a quitter. He went public against the machine, and he told voters that last month, in April 1948, the Pendergasts had warned him that there were "two strikes against me."

Strike 1—He would not deliver dead bodies exclusively to the Joe Tigerman mortuary.

Strike 2—He would not follow Pendergast orders and fire Tom Davis, his chief deputy coroner.

"The politicians were after Davis because he wouldn't send bodies to the political undertakers, either," Dr. Walker told the voters.

The coroner's office was long a political plum in Jackson County. It was considered worth upwards of twenty thousand dollars a year from the power alone to order bodies sent to favorite funeral homes, who then kicked back a gratuity to the coroner for the extra business. But Dr. Walker stood on principle. He chose to release the bodies to specific funeral homes in Kansas City that the families requested. Politics to him stopped at death's door.

Without that crucial Pendergast support he was trounced in the August primary. He showed very poorly at the polls and came in a miserable third in a three-man party contest.

But Dr. Walker left office with his head held high. He returned to private practice. Not being a pathologist, he had simply run a small coroner's office on the ground floor of the courthouse, and then later up on a fourth-floor mezzanine. He was more of a bureaucrat than a political player. But he kept his self-respect against the factions, and he knew who to turn to for medical expertise when he was faced with a death he could not easily explain.

Like this one lying now on the autopsy table. It had been brought here from the Municipal Farm to Weilert's basement, and it seemed quite suspicious to almost anyone with even the thinnest of credentials. Dr. Walker was not the kind of man to trust the sheriff's swift conclusion that the prisoner had died of mere natural causes. He was going to find out for himself what had ended the life of James Lyons. He summoned for assistance Dr. A. E. Upsher because he was the city's lead pathologist.

Dr. Upsher's widow, Mary, told me that her husband had run quite a large pathology operation in the Midwest. She said he employed about ten assistant pathologists in his Kansas City clinic and opened offices in five other states as well. At first it was too bothersome to drive to each of the sites, so he took private pilot lessons and soon flew out for visits to his clinics. "He had this big twin-engine Commander," Mary recalled. "We flew together."

He came from Oklahoma City and studied medicine in Texas and did his residency in Kansas City. As a young man he had that James Stewart kind of enthusiasm and dreamed about how he was going to change the world and make everything for the better. "He was going to paint the world," she said. "He was going to do everything to improve the world, and everybody loved him."

She was a young widow when they met. Her first husband was a World War II navy pilot, a young ensign out of Florida who was shot down over the South Pacific. "I had a month-old baby in one hand and a telegram in the other," she said.

She met Albert, as she called A. E., and they fell in love and married, and when he was working long hours performing autopsies and taking blood and tissue samples and flying off here and yon, she was doing nine holes out at the golf course. It was only at night over cocktails that they would catch up on each other's lives.

At Weilert's funeral home Dr. Upsher reviewed the heavy bruises and cuts across the dead man's torso, back, and legs. He opened the midsection but discovered no signs of heart failure, nor liver or kidney dysfunction. He searched higher, and when he opened my grandfather's throat, then they knew. The neck was broken.

So they closed him. Weilert embalmed the body. And Dr. Walker released the remains not to the Pendergast undertakers but to a funeral home of the family's choosing. His mother, Mary Lyons, chose a mortuary in Kansas City, Kansas, the Butler funeral home. From there she buried the last of her two sons.

Dr. Walker notified county prosecuting attorney James Kimbrell that my grandfather had not died of natural causes after all; rather, someone had broken his neck. "We've found enough to take action," the coroner announced. The two officials conferred, and Dr. Walker pressed Kimbrell on several key points.

He urged the prosecutor to help convene a formal inquiry; he wanted to know why the prisoner was "placed in solitary confinement in the unsanitary, black Cell No. 1." He wanted to know why city Welfare Department officials, after the body was discovered, initially tried to assure homicide detectives that the inmate probably "had the D.T.s" and could have harmed himself. But the coroner dismissed that as an unlikely scenario since the victim had not had a drink in six days. And although routine checks of prisoners in isolated cells were supposed to be made periodically, the autopsy reported that my grandfather had been dead "several hours."

With the sheriff's office dropping the ball, Dr. Walker had one last shot with the prosecutor's office for finding answers into what had happened out at the Leeds Farm and why my grandfather had not been properly cared for.

Two of his top aides, Tom Davis, still the chief deputy coroner despite how the Pendergasts felt, and Jack Gibbs, an assistant coroner, told the *Kansas City News-Press* that they were horrified that anyone would be locked up alone in the cold, steel emptiness of the jailhouse Dungeon. "It was almost unbelievably bad," Davis said. "You've never seen anything like it. A normal man would be driven insane in 48 hours in those black holes."

The paper reached Delahunty, and despite the mounting evidence to the contrary, the chief of detectives still continued to maintain there was no foul play. He dismissed the prisoner as a "habitual alcoholic," an inmate arrested for intoxication and who at the jail continued to suffer from delirium tremens shortly before his death. Probably bouncing off the walls, is how Delahunty put it.

But two private physicians, both prominent in medical circles in Kansas City, thought not. "A six-day attack of delirium tremens is possible but hardly practical," Dr. D. M. Nigro, a civic leader, told the *News-Press*. "If the deceased was in the condition reported, he should have been hospitalized rather than to have been placed in solitary confinement."

Dr. R. R. McDermott could not imagine "any reasonable conditions" in the basement cell for my grandfather to hurt himself. All that the prisoner would have had down there was the bare mattress and the waste pail. There were no pipes or rafters to swing a rope. "Such injuries might result from a fall, or by striking the spinal column against some fixture, such as plumbing fixtures," he said. "But hardly otherwise."

Drs. McDermott and Nigro had very good reasons to mistrust police investigators like Delahunty and his so-called homicide unit. Both doctors had had their own run-ins with the law; they were serious, very serious scrapes, and they both knew firsthand how the justice system in Kansas City could be manipulated against the innocent. For Dr. McDermott it nearly cost him his life.

A dozen years earlier when he was a young physician starting out in Kansas City he was charged with murdering his estranged wife. She was planning to run off with the milkman. A beauty shop employee, Thelma McDermott was shot in the chest after leaving a fashionable address in the Armour district on the arm of a tall, blond young man who drove a delivery truck for the Home Dairy Company. "We were going to get married as soon as she could get divorced," the milkman, Harold Allen, told the police. "I loved her very much."

But love can be short; love can be wistful. A few weeks after Thelma was shot the milkman married someone else.

Dr. McDermott was charged with first-degree murder, and prosecutors said they would seek the death penalty. For months he was held in the county jail awaiting trial. In all the judge allowed some half-dozen postponements. In jail the bushy-haired doctor wore wire-framed glasses and grew a sprig of a mustache.

At his trial in late 1936, Dr. McDermott testified that Allen hit and knocked him down and kicked him across the sidewalk. He said he pulled a revolver out of his pocket that he kept for safety and started firing, trying to hit Allen. "The last I remember, Allen was pushing me against a wall," he told the jurors.

The doctor said he had come to the apartment not to hurt anyone but because Thelma had told him she was pregnant, even though the estranged couple had agreed not to "run around" with others.

Dr. McDermott stepped down and awaited the verdict. The jury found him not guilty. They said he had fired in self-defense and that Thelma McDermott had been hit accidentally. The jury believed him because they found him honest and trustworthy.

"I'm going to take it easy for awhile," a relieved Dr. McDermott said upon his release from jail. "I haven't been outside for almost six months. I've just lain in bed in the cell."

Dr. Nigro also had a bad taste about law enforcement. He did not trust them, either. He was charged in federal court with improperly writing narcotics prescriptions, including thousands of half-grain morphine sulfate tablets. Some of the pills, prosecutors alleged, were given out to ex-convicts.

He was tried and convicted in 1940 of narrower charges of conspiracy and the illegal sale of only two morphine sulfate tablets. Nevertheless, the judge sentenced Dr. Nigro to four years in prison. The following year the case was thrown out when an appellate court ruled there "was no evidence of conspiracy by Dr. Nigro to violate the law." Within a month prosecutors dropped the matter.

The episode soured Dr. Nigro on the legal process in Jackson County. So when he and Dr. McDermott were asked to evaluate how the county sheriff's office seemed to be covering up for guards at the Municipal Farm in my grandfather's death, they did not hesitate to blast Purdome and Delahunty's homicide squad.

The *News-Press* carried its exposé on page 1 that Sunday, two days after my grandfather's burial. Their reporting was prompted by Claude McCandless, a prisoner at the Farm who had just been released. He headed straight for their newsroom. He based much of what he told the reporters on what he had heard and seen, and what he was told by a fireman at the Farm.

A reporter called the Kansas City branch of Alcoholics Anonymous, seeking anyone who knew something about this James Lyons. "I've been a member of A.A. for many years," one man told them, adhering to the A.A. code of refusing to give his identity. "I've known Jimmie Lyons for five years. Drunk or sober, there wasn't a nicer, politer man. It's impossible that he could've been violent. I weigh only 156 pounds, and I could, and did, handle him myself."

He said the sheriff s deputies were wrong about something else, too. "As for any statement that he had the D.T.s six days after his arrest, that's ridiculous. In six days, he'd be well on the way to recovery. I know. I've seen a lot of D.T. cases, and I've been one myself. Jimmie Lyons was beaten to death."

Scooped and embarrassed, the bigger papers hurried to catch up. The *Star* confirmed that Dr. Walker had met with Kimbrell and that further investigation by the coroner and prosecutor offices was indeed in the works. The coroner had told the prosecutor that from the autopsy there was no doubt of a broken neck, in addition to the "numerous bruises on the legs and body."

Dr. Walker also told Kimbrell that Delahunty had been wrong all along, and that he was not to be trusted. It was not natural causes, the coroner said. Murder seemed most likely the cause of my grandfather's prison death.

His aide, Charles V. Benanti, served as the coroner's attorney. He began to review the case and was told that James Lyons had been locked in solitary "after he had raised a disturbance" at the Municipal Farm. He also repeated what Delahunty had told him—that my grandfather was not a sympathetic victim and that he had in fact long been known to street patrolmen shooing drunks off skid row. "Police records on Lyons showed 80 previous arrests, many for being intoxicated," Benanti said. He added that the jail "personnel who handled Lyons would be subpoenaed to testify" as soon as officials could schedule a county coroner's inquest hearing.

With the sheriff's office unwilling to act, a corner's inquest emerged as the last shot at atonement for James Lyons, still being ridiculed as the town drunk. But proving a murder case would not be easy. Evidence would be produced and the jury would hear sworn testimony, and if everyone told the truth, particularly the guards and the prisoners and anyone else out at that Farm who might have seen or heard or known something, then they just might find the killer. When they all assembled and the inquest was convened at the downtown Jackson County Courthouse, justice for my grandfather might at last prevail.

CHAPTER 9

It is the house that Truman built. He was presiding judge of the old administrative court then. That was back in 1934, and Truman dedicated the new Jackson County Courthouse in downtown Kansas City just days before he left for Washington as the freshly elected Democratic senator from Missouri.

It too was constructed of good Missouri River–bluff limestone. The courthouse rises up from the center of the downtown business district at Twelfth and Oak streets, designed in the Art Deco style of its time, while out front stands sentry a bronze statue of gallant Andrew Jackson on horseback, the Indian fighter, duelist and president for whom the county was given its name. Old Andy Jackson was one of Harry Truman's endearing heroes.

Ages had passed from when the first Jackson County court building was a mere log house. This new one reached twenty-two stories into the clouds with electric elevators carrying visitors and county employees up and down its heights, even to the ten courtrooms where circuit judges settled into high-back reclining chairs and pounded on desks made of quartersawn oak.

The building became a monument to its people. It held the lifeblood of the community, and it recorded its history—the tax records and land grants, the marriage licenses and divorce decrees, the lawsuits and the criminal prosecutions, the sheriff's office and the county jail on the crown of the building. Anyone entering its large bronze doors and its pillared lobby of polished stone passed first under the motto carved into the front facade. It proclaimed: "The strength of the republic is not in its material wealth, but in the loyalty of its citizens who believe their government is just."

Today the city has changed in ways no one could imagine, but the courthouse remains its hall of justice.

"I dedicate this courthouse to virtue and ethical conduct," Truman said on the steps of the magnificent structure, his daughter in a group of young girls who unveiled the Jackson statue. "I dedicate this courthouse to honor and good government. I dedicate this courthouse to law and justice."

Of course, in a dozen years' time the building came to be known for something less than justice and not always ethical conduct. It was here that Sheriff J. A. Purdome ran his headquarters, and here that the two vaults were busted open on separate nights. Here too was where the sheriff's delinquent tax funds were "stolen" and the ballot boxes ripped off. And here the nine escapees torched their way out of his jail and lit the way for Purdome's defeat.

County prosecutor James G. Kimbrell also kept offices in the courthouse, a small suite on the fourth floor. A year earlier, in 1947, he had assembled a special grand jury to look into election fraud, and the panel indicted more than seventy people for trying to pad the registration rolls with "ghost" voters. He also was overseeing the investigation into the stolen ballots. It was going painfully slow.

Kimbrell had just five assistants under him, and as a Republican he was greatly outmatched in the largely predominantly Democratic county. He was a mere year and a half into his job when my grandfather died; he was the first GOP prosecutor in Jackson County in twenty years. Unlike his flashy predecessors, he liked to plead out cases rather than hold trials. He was tall and thin and wore glasses, and he was a bit of a reformer.

Soon after taking office he hired the first African American to work in a clerical capacity in the courthouse, at least as far as anyone could remember. To highlight the achievement he posed for a photograph for the black-owned *Kansas City Call* newspaper standing over Miss Erylene Bryant, she in a fashionable hat and dress, seated in front of her typewriter.

"Watch the prosecutor's office," the *Star* suggested as Kimbrell took over. "Something big is happening." That was because the local paper said there long had been an "unusual lack of gumption, lack of ability to investigate, and lack of initiative in the local prosecutor's office. Frequently local prosecutors are political whitewashers. The big test of local power is coming with Kimbrell."

By the time of my grandfather's death in May 1948, Kimbrell's office was basking in a good amount of favorable press for achieving an increase in guilty pleas from criminal defendants. He was convincing a good number of them to admit their guilt and shoulder their jail time, rather than cost the county additional taxpayer money in expensive trials and court costs. A lot of them were first offenders, and Kimbrell and his small staff were more than pleased to dispense with the cases through simple pleas of guilty. Scratch them right off the books—that was his way of doing business.

Kimbrell also sat on the local parole board, and his secretary there, Gregory Hodges, commended the prosecutor for working to clear out the caseload. "The majority of the boys have never been in trouble and they enter pleas with the idea of throwing themselves on the mercy of the court," Hodges told reporters. "They figure they have at least a 50-50 chance of getting a parole."

Kimbrell agreed. "I usually go by a man's criminal record," he said. "Age of the defendant is something else we consider. Many youths who are not criminals make mistakes. If they went to prison they would become criminals."

Kimbrell was clearing the books just as he was delaying any hearing into my grandfather's death, despite the coroner's insistence that the broken neck was evidence enough of criminal wrongdoing— manslaughter at the least, or murder under the color of authority.

But Kimbrell seemed too busy clearing other cases with guilty pleas, and almost all of the crimes he was rushing through the courts had alcohol to blame as much as anything else. Often booze seemed squarely at fault.

A typical guilty plea came in the matter of Obie McGee. He confessed he had just tried to kill his common-law wife, Elaine Wilson, on May 28. He was going to take her to the ball game that night and asked her to be dressed and have dinner ready when he arrived home. She failed on both counts, and he stormed off to the Green Duck Tavern. She chased after him.

They drank much of the evening, bottles of beer mostly, and he told police he overheard another man asking her for a date, "offering her $5." Now McGee was drinking whiskey from a bottle he purchased next door and brought back to the Green Duck. He downed two-thirds of the whiskey and chased it with more beer.

After they returned home McGee confronted Elaine with what he had heard, and "Elaine started cursing me," McGee said. From a clothes closet he pulled out a .32-caliber Smith & Wesson, turned around, and saw Elaine sitting on the bed.

"I fired one shot."

She hurried past him and started for a door.

"I fired another shot at her."

She was out the door.

He did not chase her. He went instead to another liquor store and picked up another half pint. Then he went to Union Station. "I started figuring what to do," he said. "I finally drank all this whiskey and I do not remember what happened after that." Obie McGee woke up about five in the morning in the yard by the side of his house. He hailed a cab, returned to Union Station, and bought a ticket for Odessa, Missouri.

He made Odessa by eight and purchased yet another half pint. "I walked down the railroad track where I sat down and drank this gin," he told detectives. He stayed there for about five hours, and he passed out once more.

He woke up this time realizing he was short of cash. He sold the .32-caliber to a passerby. That gave him bus fare to Sedalia, Missouri, and then on to Jackson, Mississippi. He hit Jackson on May 31 and hid out at his nephew's home on Bloom Street.

What he did not know was that Elaine had lived. He had fired twice, and he had missed twice. She went to the police, and they tracked him down at his relatives in Mississippi. They drove McGee back to Kansas City, and he stood before a judge and pleaded guilty. He was sentenced to three years.

It was another case smoothly, efficiently, promptly disposed of by prosecutor Kimbrell. Other matters he simply dropped for lack of evidence.

Isaac Jackson was out drinking one night and later said two men mugged him in a vacant lot. "They beat me until I was unconscious," he told police. "I had about three or four dollars in change in my trouser pocket." They also relieved him of his coat and pants and even his hat, he said.

At police headquarters Jackson presented the desk sergeant with a laundry receipt for the suit, a 100 percent wool coat and pants, to prove that they once were his. He named a drinking partner as one of the culprits, and officers arrested the man. But they did not find the coat, and they did not find the pants. No word on the hat.

When the case arrived at the prosecutor's office, they decided not to press charges; there would be no trial here, either. More so, they sent the defendant home and told the victim there would be no day in court. Another matter swiftly removed from the books.

So when it came to how to proceed in investigating my grandfather's death, Kimbrell the reformer passed the buck—a phrase Harry Truman hated. As Jackson County prosecutor, Kimbrell could have sent the death investigation to the county grand jury to consider a criminal indictment. He could have sent it back to Delahunty for more review into criminal charges and have him do it right this time. He could have requested an outside squad of detectives from another city or county in Missouri to take a fresh look. He could have asked state troopers to investigate. He could have done anything other than what he did.

Kimbrell the "reform" prosecutor merely opted for convening a coroner's inquest hearing. By law it was his duty to convene one if asked by the coroner, but he did not participate. Nor did he send his assistants in to collect evidence or grill witnesses. Instead, he turned the complex case over to the junior attorney assigned to the coroner's office, Charles Benanti, who seemed ill-equipped to find any criminal intent. He could call witnesses but little else. He had no real enforcement power. In the end all a coroner's jury could do was make a recommendation to Kimbrell about criminal charges if the members found the evidence to sustain one. Yet even then Kimbrell could ignore their findings. As prosecutor that all would seem fine to him, I guess; he could wipe another case away.

Inquest hearings were rather unusual back then anyway; only two had been held in the first six months of 1948. They were convened in the second-floor quarters of the county administrative court. When the testimony was taken and the evidence was in, the juries hurried off to deliberate. They usually gathered behind closed doors in a nearby judge's chambers.

Rarely could anyone remember an inquest leading to murder charges, or charges of any kind for that matter. Everyone went home free, it often seemed. Usually, the jury was done in time for lunch.

The two other inquests were held in January, and they too were completed in record time. One looked into the death of Lelon Shaw, a twenty-four-year-old World War II veteran from Chicago apparently on his way home. He died in December, shot multiple times by two policemen at Union Station after he allegedly molested a woman. He was black; she was white. The jury cleared the policemen.

Jurors in the second matter reviewed the death of Lawrence Clark. He was thirty-one, and he too had served in the last war. He was shot in the head by a night watchman about two in the morning while reportedly trying to break into the Universal Trailer Manufacturing Company on Independence Avenue.

Henry McClintock was the sixty-three-year-old night watchman, and that night he was down to the last bullet in his .22-caliber revolver. Earlier in the evening he had been shooting at rats in the warehouse. He said he was sweeping the floor when he heard Clark trying to break through a rear door. McClintock opened the door and tried to scare Clark off, and when Clark persisted he warned him a second time. Then, he said, Clark started to attack him. That was when McClintock said he fired that last bullet.

Clark collapsed in a rear alley of the building. McClintock called police. He claimed self-defense. The night watchman was white and Clark was black, and the jury sided with the watchman.

What I began to realize from these earlier coroner inquests was that the system was entrenched in county politics and that the old community mores always prevailed. Minorities and hopeless town drunks killed for whatever reason could be easily discarded in favor of policemen at the train station, night watchmen shooting rats, and guards locking up prisoners in the night.

From the start my grandfather's case was not a high priority. His inquest did not in fact begin until a month after he was buried and two days before he would have turned forty years old. But why would they want to delay the hearing and postpone solving a perplexing case in which an inmate suddenly up and died in nothing larger than a small basement closet?

The evidence was in—a broken neck. Signs of a struggle were everywhere—marks and bruises covered much of his body. No hint of an apparent suicide could be found—no rope and no bed sheets and no suicide note tucked under the bare mattress, no last words scrawled into the cell wall.

Memories would have been fresher four weeks earlier, both for the guards and for the inmates. More to the point, Delahunty's initial explanation that it appeared to be natural causes still would have been hanging ridiculously in the air. The jury could have judged that for the nonsense it was.

Why not proceed forthwith? They waited because official Jackson County was otherwise engaged. Much more important matters warranted their attention.

Sheriff J. A. Purdome, running for reelection, was busy jazzing up his campaign. He announced to voters on June 12 that his deputies would be wearing brand-new handsome uniforms—aqua colored and trimmed in dark blue. To thwart criminals they would strap on heavy black Sam Brown belts and holsters. The new duds would cost taxpayers $150 each, but Purdome pledged $750 from the sheriff's air patrol. If the county still came up short in funds, then good ol' Purdome would personally make up the difference.

Dr. James C. Walker the coroner was running hard for reelection, too, pestered by vindictive Pendergast machine toadies demanding favors, and James G. Kimbrell the prosecutor, the only Republican county official afloat in a vat of county Democrats, was merrily sweeping cases off the books.

So the hearing into the death of James P. Lyons did not open until half past nine on the morning of June 16. Thirteen witnesses, including guards and prisoners, were summoned to the courthouse. The jurors pledged to seek the truth and weigh all of the testimony and evidence. But they were done in record time. They had it all wrapped up before the noon lunch hour.

Benanti led the questioning, and first to testify was Delahunty. He said he was called to the Farm early on May 25 and that he stuck his head in the Hole and looked down at the solitary prisoner lying dead on the floor. The Hole, he said, was just eight and a half feet long, four feet two inches wide, and seven and a half feet high, more a birdcage than a jail cell. The only sanitation item, said Delahunty, was that bucket.

The homicide chief said he began interviewing jail staffers. He said he talked to inmates, too. He even went to the top of the chain of command. He said Warden Provyn told him that Fred Coleman, a guard, spotted the prisoner dead about twenty-five hours after he was placed in the cell. Delahunty said Provyn also described how the inmate earlier was in an isolation cell for treatment after suffering "a seizure, apparently epileptic," following his arrival at the jail.

Delahunty said it led him to a finding of natural causes. He said it was not until the pathologist's report identified the broken neck and the body bruises that things changed.

From the stand Delahunty tried to backpedal from what he called the "earlier misunderstanding." He said, "The report first turned in was only a dead body report. And no conclusions were drawn before knowing the pathologist's finding."

To support his position, Delahunty said "a thorough probe" was initiated at the Farm by his boss, Sheriff Purdome. He said others, including a deputy sheriff, an assistant city counselor, and Benanti, visited the Farm as well. "No evidence of mistreatment," Delahunty stated.

Provyn took the stand and confirmed what Delahunty was saying. He said there just was no other place at the Farm than solitary confinement for "violent prisoners" difficult to control.

Guards and other jail employees backed him up. Time in prison is what you make of it, they said.

Most curious of all was Lauran Thompson, the senior medical aide at the Farm. He testified that he did not know anything about whether the prisoner was suffering from epilepsy or the d.t.'s. He said his medical experience did not go that deep. But he did say the man appeared rather agitated.

Asked his professional qualifications as chief of jail medicine, Thompson said he had served twenty-two months as a navy pharmacist's mate.

"Do you have a medical degree?" asked Benanti.

"No I do not," said Thompson, though adding that he had taken several Red Cross first-aid courses.

Nevertheless, Thompson not only diagnosed the prisoner but also prescribed medicine. "Lyons was highly nervous and I gave him a half-ounce of paraldehyde [a sedative], and ordered he be given 15 grains of triple bromide later," Thompson said. "The next morning he still was highly nervous although better, and later was put in the solitary cell."

Coleman, the guard with the flashlight, said he was the one who had escorted him down to the Dungeon. He did not mention any struggle on the stairs, a fall or a crash, or even a fight to get him into the basement cell. He did not say the prisoner refused to cooperate, or resisted, or that he had to be slammed into the cell, and that that might have snapped his neck. Coleman did say he checked on the prisoner in the Hole several times over the course of the night. "He appeared to be sleeping," the guard said.

The jury was unable to assess blame. The best they could come up with was that the man died of a broken neck "from causes unknown." The jurors did include in their written finding a strong admonition that facilities at the Kansas City Municipal Farm were "wholly inadequate to care for sick patients."

There the matter was closed. Not one official took responsibility for the deplorable conditions at the Farm or the horrid scene inside the tiny solitary cell. Not one guard testified putting a hand on my grandfather.

Prisoners locked in their own cells upstairs said they could not see what was happening down below. However, several inmates said they could hear the man in the Dungeon muttering during the night. His cries occasionally floated up through the old Castle walls. One said he heard him call out, "Don't choke me."

CHAPTER 10

Every day before noon Charles B. Wheeler arrives for lunch at the Westport Flea Market restaurant. Now swallowed up by the city, the Westport neighborhood is actually older than Kansas City. It was the stepping-off point for settlers headed west to Texas and the Oregon Territory. The town of Westport was here long before there was a Fifth and Main, and today it reigns as the city's neon district, bursting with bars, restaurants, and live music. Wheeler is a medical doctor and a lawyer, and a longtime pathologist with more than a thousand autopsies under his belt. He was elected coroner in Jackson County in the 1960s. He has been a county judge, two-term mayor of Kansas City, and a Missouri state senator. He recently ran for state treasurer, but lacking enough money and statewide name recognition he came up short. At the restaurant famous for its miniburgers, curly fries, and draft beer, all of which Dr. Wheeler indulges in, he has his own table at the front window, a bronze plaque with his name on the tabletop. I'm eighty-three years old, he said. He's only eighty-two, said his wife.

Over several lunches we talked of many things, he in his gray sweater and red bow tie, listening patiently as I told him the story of the Dungeon and the guards, the bruises and the broken neck. What I wanted was a professional opinion.

The grandson of a former Jackson County coroner, he was in medical school at the University of Kansas in 1948, specializing in pathology. The names Provyn and Purdome he could not recall. He did remember Blaine Weilert and the system where coroners sent corpses to funeral directors in return for political support. When Dr. Wheeler took over as coroner in the 1960s, he said, he abolished that system. He did not think it fair. No longer were autopsies performed by outside pathologists at favored funeral homes. He conducted them himself at the city's General Hospital.

He did recall Dr. Upsher, the pathologist who uncovered James Lyons's broken neck. The two of them later were in business running a medical laboratory in Kansas City. He suggested I call Upsher's widow, Mary, in Joplin, Missouri. Maybe she had some of his old medical records.

When I reached her she said her husband hated the Kansas City politics of that era. "It was just dirty," she said. "The Democrats ruled the world." Many evenings, she said, she and her husband would unwind by sharing cocktails, he a martini, she her scotch and water. But she could not recall him mentioning the case of a prisoner from the Municipal Farm. When I tried to jog her memory, she offered only sympathy.

"An indigent drunk on the street?" she said. "How pitiful. How sad."

During another noontime lunch Dr. Wheeler described how my grandfather's body would have been examined. The marks and bruises would have been obvious, he said, and when the internal organs provided no clues, you would look directly into the dead man's face. Let him tell you, Dr. Wheeler said. There might be small marks left on the neck. Depending on how purple the marks are, you could estimate the time of death. Tiny blood vessels might have hemorrhaged in the whites of the eyes.

Then there is the neck. The neck, he said, can be fractured either by smashing the cartilage around the vocal cords, which causes you to suffocate, or breaking the bone in the back of the neck that transfixes the spinal column. Crack that bone, and death is instant. Years of alcoholism could have weakened my grandfather's bones, Dr. Wheeler said. Drunks fall a lot. But to break the back of the neck, he said, "it takes a strong man to do that."

The body would have been placed on that single porcelain table in Blaine Weilert's basement. Dr. Wheeler remembered the room; he had been there in the past. The table had drain holes to draw off the blood and water from a large rubber hose to wash the corpse. The pathologist would take a butcher knife and cut a Y-shape incision and then box cutters to cut through the cartilage. He would pull up the sternum and cut it free and then expose the organs in the midsection. "You'd have a big cavity to look into," Dr. Wheeler said.

If the kidneys or liver were shrunk, it could be from years of drinking. If the liver was yellow and fatty, it could mean alcohol. An enlarged heart or evidence of high blood pressure also could point to a lifetime on the street.

But if there is not a punctured organ or internal bleeding or proof of a heart attack, then the neck is next. The pathologist would cut open the windpipe and the muscles of the throat and inspect to see if the man was strangled. The cartilage around the larynx might be snapped, but not likely. "Sometimes just a small break will do it," Dr. Wheeler said. "But it usually requires much more. To break a man's neck you have to do it in physical battle."

He would turn the body over and remove the back spinal column and expose the spinal cord. Here is where death from a broken neck most likely would occur. But in a small, confined space like what the prisoners called the Hole and the guards the Dungeon and with nothing at your disposal, you cannot do it yourself. "Someone has to break your neck," he said. "You can't do it in a small cell like that."

Reviewing the death certificate, the inquest findings, and other documents I brought him, Dr. Wheeler complimented the coroner for disregarding the sheriff's initial findings of natural causes and pushing for his own investigation. But he said the old system of coroner inquests was equally flawed. He said inquest jurors were told only what investigators wanted them to hear and that witnesses or attorneys for the victim's family rarely were allowed to speak or offer their own opinions.

And the jurors were not always impartial, he said. When word spread that an inquest was coming, a crowd always formed outside the courthouse. People jockeyed for seats in the jury box, and for good reason. It was paid work—five or ten dollars for a few hours of sitting still. All you had to do was stay awake. Vote the right way, and you will be picked again.

Would any jury think my grandfather could have killed himself?

Dr. Wheeler laughed out loud.

Murder, then?

He offered several scenarios. The first he quickly discounted—that another inmate angry with my grandfather paid a guard to let him into the Hole. "Possible, but preposterous," the doctor said. How would a prisoner who could not afford a fifteen-dollar fine have those kinds of resources? Why would a guard risk his career? And even if he was killed by a fellow prisoner, investigators would have been more than happy to prosecute him. Even Kimbrell would have taken that kind of a case.

So a guard then, either in a scuffle getting him into the Hole or sometime after he was tossed inside, maybe because he was loud and a guard went in to shut him up. And once the man in the Hole was "discovered" dead, the guards would have quickly closed ranks. Like they testified, nobody touched him. Not a hand on him.

Dr. Wheeler cautioned me not to believe in conspiracy theories. He said they always are too complicated and too brittle, that the links in the chain never hold and that someone always breaks down. Why would everyone risk their jobs and their freedom to protect one bad apple?

He urged me to keep digging. "What goes on in the middle of the night," he said, "is anybody's guess."

Find the guards, he told me.

CHAPTER 11

The guard with the flashlight, Frederick H. Coleman, worked the overnight shift. He went out to the Farm in his khaki-brown uniform around midafternoon each day, and he did not return home until the sun was up the next morning. He was already in his late sixties by 1948, and this was just a job in retirement that he took after years toiling as a housepainter and wallpaper hanger. He was a big man, about six feet four. He weighed at times up to 250 pounds. He had blue eyes and shock-white hair and on his forearm a tattoo of a young woman's figure. To amuse his grandchildren he would flex his muscle and make the girl wiggle and dance. Fred Coleman was the one who took my grandfather to the Hole. He would have been the last to see him alive, and the first to see him dead.

City directories at the downtown library, which recorded his job as "guard, Municipal Farm," identified his wife as "Cath O." As luck would have it (for me, at least), her death certificate was among those available online, only because she has been dead fifty years or more. As it turned out, Catherine Opal Coleman died of a hemorrhage at home in November 1948, just six months after the incident at the jail. She was fifty-eight; her husband was ten years older.

Her obituary told me little. She was a housewife. She had two children; her husband had two children from a previous marriage. She was buried at the Forest Hill Cemetery, and when I telephoned the graveyard a clerk confirmed they not only had Catherine but had Frederick, too, right beside her, and that he had died in October 1970.

I pulled his obituary. He was eighty at death, and he had died at the Veterans Administration hospital in Kansas City. He was born in the small Iowa town of Guthrie Center. He was an Episcopalian. But oddly enough, the obituary did not list any occupation, a rare omission in obituaries for men. I know because I started my news-paper career writing obits. But it did note that he was a member of something called the Camp Ord Chapter of Spanish-American War Veterans. This guy was old.

At the National Archives building in Washington I found his mil-itary service record. Fred Coleman might have lived a long life, but in his youth he was quite the scrapper.

In May 1898 he was mustered into Company L of the Fiftieth Iowa Infantry. Only eighteen, he lied and said he was twenty-one. They sent him to Camp Cuba Libre in Jacksonville, Florida, where he was twice "confined" for going AWOL and twice sentenced by his field commander to "two days hard labor." He suffered from acute diar-rhea and spent days in the company hospital.

On a furlough in Des Moines he found himself in worse trouble. This time he was arrested by civil authorities at the state capital for "drunkenness and disorderly conduct." He was tried and convicted and drew fifteen days in jail—exactly as my grandfather did some years later.

Des Moines at that time had several local newspapers, yet from microfilm rolls that I reviewed I could find no mention of Coleman's arrest or conviction. I did learn that when soldiers were furloughed to Des Moines, they brought with them a good deal of trouble.

One morning several soldiers who were home on leave "tottered" into police headquarters and complained they had been robbed. One soldier leaned on a buddy's arm; another sported a bloody shirt. A second group of unnamed soldiers was arrested "after a hard night . . . of intoxication and disturbing the public quiet." A rather busy bunch, they were.

Porkey Larson was jailed for ten days for being drunk. Charles Mitchell was given "one hour to get out of town." Walter Ray drew thirty days for drinking and thirty more for carrying concealed weapons. He had been frightening pedestrians by firing off his re-volver at First and Walnut streets.

Other miscreants were not identified, and Coleman could easily have been among this crowd of soldiers, the anonymous infantry-men picked up by the police for any number of offenses fueled by alcohol.

"A few plain drunks and a couple of vagrants completed the list at the forenoon session of the court," reported the *Iowa Daily Capitol*.

"One of the prisoners arraigned for intoxication was a soldier of the regular army and claimed to have fought in the trenches at Santiago."

Coleman's sentence served in Des Moines, he was discharged from the army. He never saw action, not a battle, a skirmish, not even a forced march. He reenlisted in December 1902 and was sent to Cheyenne, Wyoming. In less than two months he came down with gonorrhea and was treated at a company hospital.

One night he sneaked away and deserted all over again. The army did not catch him for nearly a year. He was placed in military confinement, and within ten days he escaped a fourth time. It took the army nearly two years to run him to ground, and this time they hauled him in front of a general court-martial, and they convicted him of desertion. Now the army was through with Fred Coleman. He was discharged for good, and dishonorably.

Over the years he took itinerant jobs as a "home decorator." In other words, he painted houses. A grade-school dropout, his hands would have to make his living. He moved to Kansas City, and he married three times. He drank "moderately," he said, but smoked two packs of cigarettes a day and chewed tobacco. He gained weight; doctors officially listed him as obese.

Along with the tattoo of the woman's figure on his arm, he had a woman's breasts inked into the other arm and a star tattooed on his posterior. During a VA hospital exam, doctors spotted a bullet scar on his wrist, and two more on his buttocks. Since he never fought for his country, were these the souvenirs from that drunken brawl years back in Des Moines?

He was repeatedly applying for VA health benefits and free medical care. He saw VA doctors in Missouri, Virginia, and Oklahoma. Once a muscular, barrel-chested man, he came down with heart trouble and prostate problems, and he complained that he had difficulty breathing. He often could not sleep at night. His blood pressure soared, and his eyesight failed. Even his mouth was a mess—he was missing nine teeth. Seven uppers and two lowers were gone. He constantly complained that he could not work or even hold a job most of the time. By 1937 the VA agreed. They declared him 75 percent disabled, practically unable to function, let alone work.

A decade later he was employed by the City of Kansas City, and his job in May 1948 was "guarding" my grandfather.

And still Coleman was complaining about ailments. A month before he led my grandfather down to the Dungeon, Coleman again asked the VA for more hospital treatment; he was turned down. Of course, he did not dare tell them he was working at the jail. He stated he was "not employed." He likely did not want to jeopardize his monthly seventy-five-dollar disability checks.

A year after my grandfather died, in 1949, the VA records looked back at Coleman's military career and determined it was quite undistinguished. This is what the army remembered of Fred Coleman:

Rank or rating at enlistment—Private.

Battles, engagements, skirmishes, expeditions—None.

Remarks—"Character indifferent. Services poor."

I tracked down two of his grandchildren, Marguerite Ann Summers in Florida and Charles McCormick, still in the Kansas City area, in Lee's Summit, Missouri. Both are in their seventies. They loved the old man dearly, but neither remembered anything about a jailhouse death or their grandfather going downtown to testify at the courthouse. They were very nice people, and genuinely seemed shocked and saddened to learn that their grandfather had discovered my grandfather dead of a broken neck.

Summers was with her grandfather when he died in October 1960 at the Kansas City VA Hospital. By then he was an octogenarian. "He was getting married again," she said, smiling. "He went to the VA for a physical, and he went into a coma while he was there. He never regained consciousness."

She used to stay overnight at her grandparents' home in the late 1940s, after he started working what they called the "graveyard shift" out at the Municipal Farm. He was concerned about his wife being by herself at night, and he wanted his granddaughter to be on hand to keep her company. "He didn't like her to stay at home alone," she recalled.

Often he brought vegetables home from the Farm fields, and she thought that was just fine and dandy. "I loved him to death," she said.

In the back of my mind I was thinking, Okay, that's nice. But how was he at all suited or trained to properly guard prisoners, to watch over their well-being, to check on their safety in the dark of night in a pitch-black basement bunker? Here Coleman was, sixty-eight years old in 1948. He had been thrown out of the army. He had worked at various odd jobs most of his life, hanging paper and painting houses. He suffered from almost every type of physical ailment and medical catastrophe that doctors could find. According to the VA, he was 75 percent gone. How could he possibly have been qualified for this kind of work when he should have been well into retirement? He should have been at home convalescing. He should not have been anywhere near that prison Farm on the overnight shift.

So I asked her.

And she said, "I don't know how he got the job. I just know that they needed extra money, or whatever."

His grandson, Charles McCormick, also strongly defended the old man. "He was the gentlest guy I've ever been around, my grandpa," he recalled. "I never saw him in a fight in my life. He never talked about fighting anybody."

He did remember driving with his grandfather up the Farm hill to get his paycheck, climbing the winding road in the old man's 1941 dark-blue two-door DeSoto. A teenager, Charles was always made to wait in the car. "Grandpa just didn't think it was a good place for kids."

McCormick can still remember the Farm, how it appeared even then to his young, impressionable eyes, when the prison inmate count was full and the corn gleamed high on the stalk. "It kind of looked like it was run-down pretty much," he said. "It was way back up there. The buildings looked like they could use some work, and the whole place looked like it had been around a long time."

I asked him too.

"He probably got wind they needed help out there," McCormick said, struggling himself to explain why they ever hired his grandfather in his old age for what clearly became quite a stressful job at the Farm. "He probably just went out there and applied for it. And really all it was for was people who did something and couldn't pay the fine. Or driving, or speeding, and they just put them in there. I never heard him say that any of them were dangerous."

Other guards and Farm employees came there from similarly odd backgrounds, seemingly unprepared and untrained for jail work.

Harold Vetter was the chief guard during my grandfather's time at the jail. He had served in World War I and came home from Europe with an English wife and a dream of a career on the stage. He starred as an actor and musician in local productions around Kansas City. With his wife, Elaine, and Vivian, an older brother, they toured together in a traveling show company. But fame would not be theirs.

By 1930 the Great Depression had drawn the curtain on such entertainments, and the stage no longer commanded the paying audiences of old. Vetter's father, August Eugene Vetter, a city inspector in Kansas City, helped Harold land a job out at the Farm. There he stayed until around 1960, when at retirement age he and Elaine left Kansas City and moved to Los Angeles.

For a while he worked as a school repairman, and then he died in 1968 of heart disease at the VA Hospital in Los Angeles. His story ended at the Eternal Valley Memorial Park Cemetery in eternally sunny California. For all I could tell he left no survivors. There was not even a newspaper obituary to mark his passing.

Wendell L. Smith served as a school superintendent in De Soto, Missouri, before he came to work as a clerk at the jail. He died in Kansas City in 1962. I found a grandson in Grain Valley, Missouri, Jeffrey A. Smith, but he was just a month old when they lost his grandfather.

His years in the education system and as a jail clerk taught him to be meticulous about saving just about everything. His starched U.S. Navy uniform was packed safely away in the attic. His old set of tools were boxed up and stored, too. The grandson in Grain Valley thought there might be some papers left, maybe files and records even. His grandfather, Jeffrey Smith said, was known to keep notes and letters about his life, and maybe he jotted down a thing or two about the Farm, his impressions if nothing else. Maybe a death in the jail basement bothered him enough to put his thoughts on paper. He was that diligent about holding on to history.

"He was real precise," Jeffrey Smith told me. "He might have kept a diary. He was very well organized." He promised to prowl through his mother's attic, where anything like that would likely have been kept after all these years, sixty years now. He promised to let me know. Nothing turned up.

I last turned to Lauran Thompson, the chief medical aide who admitted on the witness stand that despite his limited medical training he had repeatedly sedated my grandfather. He also was a veteran; his war was the one just won in Europe against the Third Reich. Unlike the other jail guards and staff at the Farm, medicine and not jailing would be his calling. And he was only a year younger than my grandfather.

Thompson was born in Iowa and raised in Des Moines. In 1923 he married a Missouri woman, and they settled in Kansas City. For a while he worked as a clerk for a mail-order house and started a family. He was tall and dark with brown hair and brown eyes.

His mother had been a music teacher, and she taught him to sing and play the piano. But a doctor was what he always hoped to become. As a boy he would carry around a leather doctor's kit. It was, he said, his calling.

In 1940 the Farm took a chance and hired him as a nurse. A year later he was the assistant medical aide at the jail, and he moved his family into one of the staff homes on the jail property. Soon he was chief of medicine. Guards drove his daughters to school. They built the girls a wooden slide for them to play on. Prisoners tended to the Thompson family garden while he ran the jail clinic. He mostly treated small problems and medicated some of the prisoners down with colds or fevers. He sent major cases to the city's public medical complex on Hospital Hill near the downtown area.

Thompson enjoyed his work but feared he was getting too old for medical school. He worried time was passing him by. Then another interruption slowed him down. The navy took him during the later years of World War II, and medical school seemed to be slipping from his future.

He came home from the war and returned to his job at the Farm. But this time he did not live there. He bought an old house in the city, a hundred years old, they said, and he fixed it up and rented out one side for thirty-five dollars a month. He took a second job at a laundry, pressing suits.

Finally, he quit the Farm and the cleaners and started school as a student at the Kansas City College of Osteopathy. Mildred, his wife, went to work at the cleaners. She bought a bicycle to get around because a car was out of the question. They could not afford the newspaper or a television either, and so at night, when Thompson put down his school medical books and rubbed his eyes, for he studied hard, the family gathered around the radio with a bowl of popcorn.

At last the dream came true for Lauran Thompson. He graduated in 1952 with honors as president of his senior class. Now-Dr. Thompson moved his family out to Oklahoma, and there he took a prestigious position in medical care and treatment for a large firm, the Phillips Petroleum Company. He became director of the company's Executive Medical Department, and in 1973 he retired.

Thompson was a Shriner and a Mason, and for twelve years he served as president of the Crippled Children's Association. He split his last years between Sun City, Arizona, and Bartlesville, Oklahoma. He died in 1984 at the Jane Phillips Hospital in Bartlesville, after a long illness, and his daughter, Carole Trusler, loves him still. "My father was a kindhearted man," she told me.

I found her after collecting death certificates, obituaries, and credit reports, and reviewing old census records and other documents. Her mother was gone, too. Carole was living in Oklahoma, the last of the Thompson family, and she was quite startled when I telephoned her one weekday evening. She was at home frying taco meat for an upcoming church dinner, and was immediately suspicious why anyone would be inquiring about something that happened so long ago. "I find this so strange," she said when I began to tell what happened to my grandfather. "I'm getting a stomachache just hearing this."

So she fired questions at me.

Was I an attorney? She does not like lawyers.

Was I taping our conversation? She did not want to be recorded.

"What are you trying to prove?" she demanded. "Are you accusing someone of murder? My father never hurt anyone. He never even spanked his kids."

We spoke for an hour. I told her about the death in the Hole and her father's testimony. She said she was thirteen at that time, and she recalled nothing of the case or her father's trip downtown to the courthouse where he took the stand as a key witness in the inquest.

"He only medicated some of the guys who needed it," Carole told me. "If they were really sick, they took them to the Kansas City General Hospital."

I asked if perhaps her family had saved any records from her father, a diary maybe. She told me nothing was left.

"I'm really sorry about your grandfather," she said. "But if my grandfather was in jail, why would I want anyone to know it? I'm a kindhearted woman. My father was a kindhearted man. I'm an honest person. I'm a church person."

I tried to press her more, gingerly explaining that my grandfather was born Catholic and buried out of a Catholic church and that his only crime at the end of his life was that he drank far too much and was found by the police passed out on the street.

He could not pay the fine because he did not have the fifteen dollars. And he did not have the fifteen dollars because he drank more than he worked, if he worked at all. And he could not start working again because he could not stop drinking. He could never stop drinking. My grandfather, our grandmother told us when we were small, was just a lovable old drunk. And his life cycled out of control. For that and only that, somebody somehow killed him.

"I feel awful about your grandfather," Carole said. "That's no reason for somebody to die."

Then I told her one thing more, that I was searching as much for my mother as I was for myself.

"I promise you," she said, "whatever happened my father was not involved. I am a good Christian, and I can tell you that is true. Whoever did this, God will reckon things. If somebody killed him, they will pay for it. God will take care of everything. God takes care of all of us."

She paused. "He also forgives," she said.

And she was right.

CHAPTER 12

And then I knew I was done. Because even though I never quite realized it, it was some kind of an inner peace that I been searching for all along. I had embarked on a journey hoping to find a grandfather and maybe his killer too but had instead discovered something of much more value. I had unearthed a dark side of my family that I never dared dream existed, and through them I inherited a new understanding about myself.

His absence had helped shape me into the man I became because long ago I had learned how to live without grandparents. If he was never a part of my past how could he be a part of me now?

His presence today in my life only helped unlock the riddle of his death. It did not ease the pain of his departure. Not in leaving this world but in leaving my grandmother and my mother in the first place. In leaving us all.

So I realized that the doctor's daughter was correct. I should let it go. It was time to let it go. And I did.

I gathered up the old court records and the census tracts and the newspaper clippings and stuffed them away. I did not go back to the caves, and I did not drive up the hill to visit again the fields of the old Farm. I did not go back to Fifth and Main and hope I might imagine my grandfather alive again in my world. He was never coming back because for me he never was.

There was something I did do. I took another long look at the old photograph of James Patrick Lyons decked out in his suit and his tie, from the time he married my grandmother and celebrated in that field or backyard or wherever it was. I saw again what my family says is my own image, my look-alike, the man strong and self-confident in the picture but also wary that hard times are ahead. I placed it back into the box and put the box back on the closet shelf. I put it all away.

I picked up the power of forgiveness.

Against the long arc of time I had probably gotten as close as possible to what had happened. He went from the bottle to the jail to solitary confinement and in the end to his final prison, the tomb. For me I would have to leave it to dust that someone snapped my grandfather's neck or tossed him down that flight of stairs. If someone in the night opened the Dungeon door and smashed him against the wall, then so it was.

That is past. That is history. Like I said, our strength comes from the things that remain.

And even if he were here today and he knew how I felt, what would he say? What could he say? There is shame in all of us, and for many it can be a mighty bitter cocktail, too strong a drink for even the strongest of men.

Only in my head can I imagine him trying to face me, wobbly and not sturdy enough to explain his life. I expect he would just wink at me with that thin, bloodshot eye, slur a few words in the brogue his parents bequeathed him, and turn his head in embarrassment. Let the whiskey do his talking.

A wink and the brogue and a head turned away.

He speaks. "I'm sorry, son. I drinks a bit."

In the spring sixty years after my grandfather died, when he would have been one hundred years old had he lived and had he behaved, I drove once more out to the cemetery. Looking down at his headstone I cleansed my heart. I told him I bore him no grudge for his wasted life; I forgave him the pain he caused our family, the hurt he caused others. Time heals. Sixty years wipes it away. I like to think he is in heaven, if only because there are no guards in heaven. Or maybe he waits in purgatory. That is a jail, too, but with a safe way out. So I thought: Let's raise a toast, let's fill our cans, let's be Irish eyes a-smiling. At last I've found my grandfather, and quite the bum he was. Hallelujah, he's a bum.